JODHPUR LANCERS

A.C. LOVETT

JODHPUR LANCERS

MICHAEL CREESE

The Mehrangarh Museum Trust, Jodhpur

Lustre Press
Roli Books

Page 2: A Jodhpur Lancer from a watercolour by Major A.C. Lovett.

Several cannon captured by the Jodhpur Lancers in foreign wars continue to adorn the ramparts of Mehrangarh Fort.

To the officers, non-commissioned officers and men of the Sardar Risala/Jodhpur Lancers

1889 *to* 1951

'RAN BANKA RATHORE!'

(THE RATHORE - INVINCIBLE IN BATTLE!)

CONTENTS

Facing page: Trumpet banner of the Jodhpur Lancers, today at the Umaid Bhawan Palace.

His Highness the Maharaja with a Jodhpur Lancer cap badge.

Writing has rarely given me greater pleasure and satisfaction, and I consider it a profound and poignant honour to be able to pen the foreword to this splendid book as we enter the centenary year of my Family Regiment's finest hour.

It is said that no military annal, no history of war, is quite complete without the Charge of the Jodhpur Lancers at Haifa on 23 September 1918. Indeed, it is described by many as 'perhaps the greatest cavalry action ever on a regimental scale'.

But in fact, in no more than the seven decades of their formal existence, the Jodhpur Lancers covered themselves in glory on many battlefields; as far apart as Tirah in Afghanistan to Shimanzai in China; from Ncuvc-Chapcllc and Cambrai in Francc to Haifa in Palestine, Aleppo in Syria and Basra in Iraq. True to a man, the JL encapsulated the very essence of over a thousand years of warrior tradition and martial spirit of my clan, the Rathore – famed and feared as 'Invincible in Battle'.

Due to various and different reasons on both sides, the contribution, heroism and sacrifice of the Indian Army in the two world wars has largely been forgotten. The story of the Jodhpur Lancers is no different and has remained untold outside of Jodhpur and Marwar. I therefore congratulate, and am most grateful to Dr Michael Creese, an amateur military historian in the finest mould, for this book, which not only sets the record straight but will also, I am confident, inspire many more regimental histories.

It is also most timely. It is over a hundred years now since countless young men from India first crossed the seas to join an event of truly global proportions. Many of them never came back. A few years ago I paid tribute at a Jodhpur Lancers memorial in Heliopolis, Cairo. To see the names of some of these men from the villages of Marwar carved in stone in a faraway land was profoundly moving. It is a matter of great pride for all of us that no less than the prime minister of India himself recently bowed his head at the memorial of Major Thakur Dalpat Singh, the commanding officer of the Jodhpur Lancers, revered as the Hero of Haifa.

A century later, as we strive still to define our national identity, and to come to terms with it; we should not trouble ourselves with the colour of the flag these gallant men fought and died for. All we need to remember now, and to salute them for, is that they fulfilled their Dharma.

Maharaja Gaj Singh II of Marwar-Jodhpur

ACKNOWLEDGEMENTS

Loving India, and Rajasthan in particular, I am delighted to have been given this opportunity to make a small contribution to the record of the country's long and varied history in the form of this story, which could not have taken shape without the support and goodwill of many people. First and foremost, I am indebted to His Highness the Maharaja of Jodhpur, who has not only supported and encouraged this enterprise throughout but also given me access to his private archives and permission to reproduce many of the photographs included in this work.

Any historian must acknowledge the work of those who have gone before. It was most unfortunate that no regimental history of the Jodhpur Lancers was prepared at the end of the First World War – indeed, that is one reason for writing the present volume. The closest we have come to such a history are two booklets: *A Short History of the Services Rendered by the Imperial Service Troops during the Great War 1914–18* by Major General Sir Harry Watson, and the *History of the 15th (IS) Cavalry Brigade during the Great War 1914–18*, published anonymously by the Stationery Office in London. Fortunately, the gap in the history was realized at the end of the Second World War, and the *History of the Jodhpur State Forces in the War 1939–45* by Major General R.C. Duncan gives a full account of that period.

Facing page: Watercolour of Sir Pratap by Major Alfred Crowdy Lovett, 1911.

I have drawn heavily on these three volumes in the present work. Also useful has been the booklet *Jodhpur's Contribution to Victory*, published by the Government Printing Press in Jodhpur in 1945.

Further details of the Lancers at war can be gleaned from the First and Second World War diaries of the regiment, held in the Public Record Office at Kew, although, unfortunately, those for the Second World War are not complete. The reports of the chief censor of Indian Mails in the Oriental and India Office Library at the British Library contain translations of extracts from letters written by a number of Jodhpur Lancers who served in France in the First World War. The library of the National Army Museum in Chelsea holds a collection of the letters of Eustace Maxwell, who served as captain with the Jodhpur Lancers in France from 1914–15. Some of Major Hervey's letters home (he was brigade major of the 15th IS Cavalry Brigade) were published in the *Journal of the Royal United Services Institute*.

A number of retired Lancers very generously gave their time to share with me their reminiscences and often brought along medals and other militaria, some of which are illustrated in this book. For this I am indebted to Lieutenant Colonel Prabhu Singh, Lieutenant Colonel Virendra Singh (son of Lieutenant Colonel Dalpat Singh), Captain Rao Raja Bijai Singh (grandson of Sir Pratap Singh), Risaldar Major and Honorary Captain Umed Singh, Risaldars Bishan Singh, Govind Singh and Madho Singh, Dafadar Clerk Prem Singh, and Sowars Hanuman Singh and Parbhu Singh. The following descendants of the Jodhpur Lancers also contributed freely in helping to build up a picture of the regiment: Colonel Mal Singh (grandson of Amar Singh), Lieutenant Colonel Daulat Singh, 15th Rajputs (grandson of Risaldar Mohabbat Singh and son of Colonel Dungar Singh MC of the Jodhpur Infantry), Thakur Jayendra Singh (son of Brigadier Hari Singh), and Thakur Manohar Singh (son of Brigadier Zabar Singh – the last commanding officer of the Jodhpur State Forces).

Anyone writing on the Indian State Forces must pay tribute to the pioneering work of Richard Head and Tony McClenaghan, and I was fortunate enough in being able to read a copy of Richard's early volume on the Jodhpur Lancers. I am particularly indebted to Shri Ranjit Singh, the secretary of the Brigadier Zabar Singh School, for giving me a copy of his notes on the history of the regiment. Kunwar Gajendra Singh equally generously gave me a copy of his notes on the career of his great, great grandfather – Colonel Thakur Pratap Singh. Shobha Kanwar Baiji kindly provided me with a copy of the letter from Captain Hervey to Mrs Tudor explaining the circumstances of Dalpat Singh's death. The diary of Amar Singh, who served as a risaldar with the Lancers in China in 1900, provides us with a first-hand account of that campaign. I am most grateful to the late Thakur Mohan Singhji of Kanota for giving me access to that part of Amar Singh's diary, together with permission to quote from it and to reproduce some of the photographs of that period. His sons, Man Singh and Prithvi Singh, have been equally helpful and supportive. Dr Kunwar Mahendra Singh, director (Culture) of the Mehrangarh Museum Trust, gave me access to the archives stored in the fort. Colonel Karan Singh (lately the Poona Horse) very kindly arranged a most pleasant evening in what had once been the officers' mess of the Jodhpur Lancers and is now a divisional headquarters mess.

In England the various staff of the Oriental and India Office Library at the British Library, the Library of the National Army Museum and the Public Record Office, Kew have all played an important role in helping locate the relevant material. Material from the Royal Archives at Windsor appears by gracious permission of Her Majesty Queen Elizabeth II. I am grateful to Mrs J. Kelsey, deputy registrar at the Royal Archives, for her assistance in locating material pertaining to Sir Pratap Singh and to the Jodhpur Lancers. It has not proved possible to locate the copyright holders for the letters of Major Hervey or Colonel Maxwell. I am also grateful to Mr Simon Wood, assistant archivist at Eastbourne College, for his assistance in providing material on Dalpat Singh's time there and to the headmaster for his permission to reproduce some of that material, including plates. I also wish to express my gratitude to the staff of the Commonwealth War Graves Commission, both in Maidenhead and in Arras, for their assistance in locating the graves of the Jodhpur Lancers in France. Philip Magrath, curator of artillery at the Royal Armouries, Fort Nelson, very kindly provided me with information about the origins of the 'Haifa cannon' and Melvyn Jeremiah CB JP, secretary of the Heraldry Society, identified the coat of arms on these. Craig Bowen, the assistant curator of the Royal Engineers' Museum at Chatham, equally helpfully gave details of the involvement of the sappers at Haifa.

Had it not been for the hard work and enthusiasm of Kanwar Dhananajaya Singh (a great, great grandson of Sir Pratap), this book would perhaps never have been written. It was his response to my initial enquiry about the Jodhpur Lancers which led to our visit to Jodhpur, and he took considerable pains to locate material and to arrange interviews with all those noted above. His kindness and support all through the project have indeed been invaluable. My wife and I are most grateful to him and to his father Rao Raja Mahendra Singh for their delightful hospitality during our stay in Jodhpur and for many of the photographs and portraits from his family's archives. My friend and fellow Indian Army enthusiast, Dr Mike Thomas, read a draft of the book and made a number of helpful comments. Priya Kapoor of Roli Books has also made a number of very helpful comments on the text. Neelam Narula has been a most patient editor who has clarified the text in a number of places. I am also pleased to have this opportunity to acknowledge my debt to the late F.E. Watson Esquire, my history teacher at Culford School, who first encouraged my study of military history. Finally, I must pay tribute to my wife, Lesley, whose encouragement led me to write to HH the Maharaja of Jodhpur in the first place. Together we have made many friends in India and Lesley has been an enthusiastic ally throughout the research and writing, reading drafts, making very helpful suggestions and driving me around the highways and byways of northern France. Together we visited the final resting place of every Jodhpur Lancer buried in France, with the exception of six who are buried in Marseille. Without the help and willing cooperation of all of those named above, this book would never have been written. As with any author, however, the responsibility for any errors rests with me alone.

MICHAEL CREESE

Stratford St Andrew, Suffolk, 2018

Facing page: Jodhpur Lancers epaulette badge.

J L

INTRODUCTION

'As soldiers the Rathores were second to none. Tradition and the desert landscape round their villages had endowed them with the toughness and self-discipline so necessary to a cavalry soldier.'

MAJOR J.D. SHEBBEARE
The Poona Horse

There can be few people alive today who have witnessed a cavalry charge and even fewer, if any, who have taken part in one. Many of the famous regiments – amongst them the Jodhpur Lancers, the Gwalior Lancers, the Mysore Lancers – whose lance pennons fluttered above the dusty plains of India, are no more. Only the President's Bodyguard and the 61st Cavalry survive to carry on the proud tradition of the Indian sowar on his horse, a tradition which can be traced back to at least the seventh century AD. In the regiments which still exist, such as the Poona Horse, the troopers are mounted in armoured cars and tanks. However, the

Facing page: An NCO of the Jodhpur Lancers – A watercolour by Major A.C. Lovett.

stirring deeds of their predecessors in the past may be in danger of being lost in the mists of time. Who, for instance, would now remember that Indian cavalry regiments served with great distinction for three years in the mud and blood of France during the First World War; that the charge of the Jodhpur Lancers at Haifa in 1918 was one of the very last great cavalry charges in history; that they displayed all the dash and elan of the Polish Lancers at Somo-Sierra, and the steely determination of Cromwell's Ironsides at Marston Moor? Yet the capture of the defended town of Haifa by cavalry – an event unique in military history – remains almost entirely overlooked and unheard of outside Jodhpur.

It is said that old soldiers never die; that they merely fade away. Whether or not that is true, it is important that their history be preserved and not allowed to fade away or be forgotten, for there is much to gain from the legacy of the sheer grit and determination of the Lancers, from their sense of duty to the state and to their country, because courage, honour and service are as relevant today as they were ever before. The British nicknamed the Jodhpur Lancers 'The Jo Hokums' – the term 'Hokum' in this case implies respect and 'Jo Hokum' may be interpreted as 'Yes Sir', 'As You Order' or simply 'Can Do'. The unquestioning loyalty of the Lancers to their maharaja was unrivalled.

Amar Singh was born in Jaipur but was sent to Jodhpur to be educated under the supervision of Sir Pratap Singh. As part of his education he started writing a diary, a practice which he continued through his life. The diary is now preserved at his home at Kanota, near Jodhpur. He served with the Jodhpur Lancers in China in 1900 as a squadron commander, before joining the prestigious Imperial Cadet Corps. He then served as a staff officer in France and wrote a note in his diary in 1915 about the importance of keeping records. He felt that it was important for each nation to keep its own records of the experiences of its soldiers and that although British historians would write accounts of the Great War, the Jodhpur Lancers would likely receive only a passing mention. Amar Singh did begin to write some notes for a projected article on the regiment, but sadly, this was never published. He believed that poetry was the best form in which records ought to be kept because this was the manner in which the deeds of past Indian heroes had been handed down to succeeding generations. Unfortunately, the present writer is no poet; nevertheless he hopes that this book will serve as a permanent memorial to the men who served their state and their country so faithfully and so well.[1]

To appreciate the story of the Jodhpur Lancers, one must first understand the people of Jodhpur and their traditions. Jodhpur is one of the princely states of Rajasthan (formerly Rajputana), a vast area lying to the south-west of Delhi and stretching as far as the border with Pakistan and including the Thar Desert. The great kingdoms of Rajasthan were ruled by princely clans whose chiefs were called *rajas*, the word *rajput* simply meaning son of a raja. The Rajputs are a proud warrior race. As the travel writer Louise Nicholson puts it, 'They make no bones about their pedigree; they claim to be descended from the sun and moon via the hero gods of the Ramayana and Mahabharata.' Colonel James Tod, in his *Annals and Antiquities of Rajasthan*, first published in 1829, equates the feudal structure of Rajput society with its clan organization to that existing in England immediately after the Norman Conquest. The Rajputs played a significant role in Indian history: 'In the centuries immediately preceding and following the Muslim conquest of India, the Rajputs were destined to play an often heroic and always pivotal role.'[2] Their territories would eventually stretch far beyond Rajputana and would constitute the most numerous of the princely states during the British Raj. To the British the Rajputs represented the quintessence of all that was admirable in India's martial traditions, and Sir Pratap Singh, three times regent of Jodhpur, was the paradigm of this ideal. 'The Rajputs made war like gentlemen; there was chivalry in their combats and their rules of war were honourable.'[3]

Amar Singh in the full dress of the Imperial Cadet Corps.

The harsh and inhospitable land of Marwar, which included Jodhpur, Bikaner and seven smaller states in the western and north-western area of Rajasthan, was under the control of one particular warrior clan, the Rathores. In 1947, at the time of Indian Independence, Jodhpur was the third largest of the Indian princely states with an area of over 36,000 square miles, larger than, for instance, Belgium. Marwar State and the city of Jodhpur were founded in 1459, when the building of the Mehrangarh Fort commenced. However, the standard of the Rathores had been planted in the sand hills of the Luni as far back as in 1212. The first Rathore ruler was Rao Sheoji, who enjoyed a considerable reputation as a warrior of great courage and strength – a reputation which his descendants would build upon and enhance. The original Mehrangarh fortress was much smaller than the magnificent edifice that exists today. As the Rathores became more and more powerful, the fortress – a symbol of their wealth and importance – expanded. Their golden age was the second half of the fifteenth and the first half of the sixteenth century, during which period they emerged as one of the most powerful clans in India and they 'ruled as sovereign kings, undisputed, unchallenged, independent.'[4] The nineteenth Rathore ruler, Rao Maldev, was described as the most potent prince in Hindustan. The head of the clan Jodha, primus inter pares (first amongst equals), he ruled through Thakurs who were accountable to him for one or more villages, and on whose goodwill and support he depended. It was this system which provided much of the clan's vigour and vitality in the early years, but this very system would eventually prove largely responsible for its later downfall as clan fought with clan. This often intense rivalry was ultimately to prove disastrous. As Tod put it, 'They were never capable of uniting, not even for their own preservation!'

The regiment known as the Sardar Risala, or Jodhpur Lancers, officially came into being only in 1889, but the unit can trace its lineage back to as far as 1212 when the ruler Rao Shinajee formed a personal bodyguard at Khair, the then capital of the state of Marwar. This bodyguard continued through the centuries under various names and under the personal command of successive rulers, helping to enlarge the territorial limits of the state. The regiment fought at the Battle of Panipat in 1526 against the army of the great Mughal emperor Babur and in 1527, at Kanua, when the Rathores for the first time came up against artillery fire. 'This battle marks a watershed in their power because, from now onwards, the gun would rule the battlefield and the Rathore cavalry with their lances and swords would find themselves increasingly ineffective in warfare. To the very end, however, they would prefer "the breathless intoxication of a cavalry charge."'[5]

A large Rathore army, led by Maldev, was defeated by the Afghans under Sher Shah at the Battle of Sammel in 1544. This, it is said, was only due to dissension in their ranks induced by Sher Shah. However, in spite of their defeat at Kanua, the Rathores were able, through their spirit and skill-at-arms, to maintain their power and importance throughout the reigns of the great Mughal emperors. For instance, Jaswant Singh, another distinguished general, rendered brilliant services for the Emperor Aurangzeb in Kabul and won for himself the title of Maharaja. On the eve of the Battle of Dharmatpur in 1658 he was advised to capture the enemy cannon in the dark but scornfully replied, 'We Rathores fight during the day – only rats forage at night.' In the event, 10,000 of his men died the next day and only nightfall brought an end to the struggle between Rajput courage and artillery shells. Other Rajputs acted as governors and viceroys for the Mughal emperors, gathering much wealth as they did so.

Unfortunately, Jaswant Singh died in 1678 without an heir, although two of his wives were pregnant at the time of his death. Aurangzeb seized the opportunity to take possession of Jodhpur. However, the two wives each gave birth to a son and the elder child, Ajit Singh, was regarded by the Rathores as their rightful ruler. The boy was smuggled out of Jodhpur by his faithful nurse, who left her own child behind so that his cries would deceive the besiegers into thinking that the future ruler was still present in the fort. Ajit Singh's bodyguard protected the future maharaja throughout the thirty-year war of Rathore Independence and eventually helped him regain the throne of Marwar on Aurangzeb's death in 1707. During the second half of the eighteenth century the state was ravaged by incursions from the powerful Marathas of Scindia and by civil war as clan fought clan. Finally, in 1787, the Rathores faced a Maratha army trained by a Frenchman, General Benoit de Boigne at Tunga, a village north of Marwar. 'Rathore valour shone forth in all its glory charging the dense lines of de Broglie, sabring his artillerymen at their guns and compelling Scindia to abandon not only the field but all his conquests.' The Rathores' victory here was all the more significant because this was the first time they faced an army trained in

Mehrangarh Fort, the fort of Jodhpur, in the late 1800s.

Cannon on the ramparts of Mehrangarh Fort overlooking the city, 1908.

the modern techniques of war. Three years later, James Skinner, the founder of Skinner's Horse – the premier cavalry regiment in the Indian Army – was present at the Battle of Malpura in 1800 and spoke of the Rathores' charges: 'The brisk walk quickening into a trot, breaking into a canter, flowing into a full-blooded gallop, the ominous rumble, the different flags of the Thakurs, the flash of sword and lance, the cry of four thousand saffron clad men – Ran Banka Rathore!' Saffron was the traditional colour worn by Rajputs who had vowed to seek either victory or death and who went out arrayed like a bridegroom to his wedding ceremony. At the murderous battles of Patan and Merta in 1790, Rajput courage was once again heroically but fruitlessly displayed against European tactics and their significantly superior numbers.

In 1818 a treaty was concluded with the British whereby Maharaja Man Singh agreed to put at the former's disposal a body of 1,500 cavalrymen. Unfortunately this was never an effective force and the requirement was later changed to an annual payment of Rs 115,000 towards the European-led Jodhpur Legion. Enlistment into this unit commenced in January 1836 under a Captain Downing and in November the same year the troops moved to Erinpura in southern Marwar. This force originally consisted of three troops of cavalry and four companies of infantry, which later increased to eight companies with two camel-drawn nine-pounder guns. The unit did good service in Merwara in 1839 but later – with the exception of the Bhil companies – joined in the rebellion of 1857. The Bhil companies subsequently formed the nucleus of the Erinpura Corps.

Before India's independence in 1947, one quarter of the population of India lived in the princely states under their hereditary rulers, and British rule extended to only half of India's total area. These rulers, in agreement with the British, maintained forces which varied considerably in size and effectiveness. The smallest states would provide them with what was, in effect, little more than an ill-trained ceremonial guard while the larger ones, such a Hyderabad and Mysore, would have several effective regiments at their disposal. The threat of Russian invasion through Afghanistan in 1885 prompted a number of the rulers to make elements of their forces, to be known as Imperial Service Troops, available to the Government of India in times of war. In return, the government would contribute towards the cost of equipping these units, which as per expectations would be up to the same standard of training as the infantry and cavalry regiments of the Indian Army, and fully able to fight alongside them. Training was supervised by officers seconded from the Indian Army; schools of instruction were set up and officers from the Imperial Service units were seconded from time to time to units of the Indian Army in order to broaden their experience.

Sir Pratap Singh, then regent of Jodhpur, embraced the Imperial Service scheme whole-heartedly and the Sardar Risala was formed in Jodhpur in 1889. General Sir Frederick Roberts ('Bobs'), commander-in-chief in India visiting Jodhpur for the first time in 1889, spoke at a banquet given in his honour and quoted Colonel Skinner: 'If we seek for a picture of chivalrous gallantry, unswerving fidelity and fearless self-devotion, we have only to turn to the cavalry of the Rajput states, and particularly to that of the Rathores. It is the Izzat (honour) of the Rajput which is dearer to him than life and which makes him ready to sacrifice everything in defence of his chief and clan.... We may rest satisfied that no Rajput cavalry will be more self-sacrificing or more loyal to their rulers than the body of Rathore horse now being raised at Jodhpur.'[6]

All regiments are, to a greater or lesser degree, like a family business with son following father, nephew following uncle into the ranks. However, because of the clan system inherent in Rathore society, there was a particularly strong and keen sense of family amongst the Jodhpur Lancers. Such was the prestige of the regiment that even the position of syce (groom) was sought after – in spite of all the hard work that such a job entailed in a crack cavalry regiment. Philip Mason, one of the most perceptive writers on the Indian Army, quotes Captain Bingley, who served in a Rajput infantry regiment: 'Rajputs are soldiers by tradition and are taught by their religion to regard the profession of arms as their legitimate occupation.' Mason refers to a personal and hereditary idea of service which was stronger in Rajasthan than anywhere else in India and is not unlike that of the Scottish clansman who looked towards his clan chief for protection, in return for which he gave him his loyalty and devotion.[7]

Whether or not in the Imperial Service Scheme, the State Forces were officered by Indians who could hold any rank up to general within that force, depending on the whim of the ruler; in the Jammu and Kashmir force, for instance, the lowest commissioned rank prior to 1928 was that of major. On active service, British officers were seconded to the units. Unfortunately, there were no training facilities for the states' officers until the opening of the Indian Military Academy in 1932 when ten places were reserved for cadets from the princely states. Pay and pensions were generally less in the State Forces and there was a relatively small pool of men with the right qualities and experience to become officers. Many of the State Forces saw very little, if any, action and the routine of a garrison was unappealing and did little to aid recruitment. In the Second World War, the Indian States Forces Officer Cadet School was established, which enhanced the quality of officers significantly.

Troops from Hyderabad fought alongside British soldiers during the suppression of the Great Mutiny of 1857 and men from the same state also went to Burma in 1885. Contingents from a number of the states took part in the wars

Sir Pratap at a ceremony during the viceroy Lord Hardinge's visit to Jodhpur, 1916.

on the North-West Frontier in 1897 and 1900. Troops from Jodhpur and three other states went to China in 1900 accompanied by Sir Pratap Singh. At the start of the First World War in 1914, twenty-nine states were involved in the scheme, with a total of over 22,000 men under arms. State Forces served in the Middle East, Gallipoli, Mesopotamia and East Africa but the Jodhpur Lancers were the only cavalry regiment to serve in France on the Western Front. During the Great War, Imperial Service troops provided over 18,000 men for active service. Of these nearly 2,000 were killed or wounded and they were granted over 700 awards, including a number of Military Crosses awarded for outstanding bravery. However, the war revealed that the wide variation in organization between the State Forces produced difficulties, and in 1920 the conditions of service were revised. A number of units, termed Field Service Units and including the Jodhpur Lancers, would be armed and organized exactly as other regiments of the Indian Army and such units would be unconditionally available in time of war. A second tier of General Service Units would be supplied with arms and equipment at cost price and might be placed at the disposal of the government while, finally, there were also some militia units with a lower standard of equipment and training. Forty-nine states were now involved with a total of over 50,000 men. Training would be supervised by British military advisers under the eye of a military adviser-in-chief.

In the Second World War, State Forces fought bravely alongside their regular counterparts in the Western Desert, Italy and Burma, gaining over 200 awards for bravery. Captain M.K. Durrani of the Bahawalpur Infantry was awarded the George Cross, equivalent to a Victoria Cross, for his courageous behaviour while he was a prisoner of the Japanese in Malaya. After Independence, the State Forces were either disbanded or, like the Jodhpur Lancers, were absorbed into the Indian Army. Field Marshal Sir Claude Auchinleck, the last and greatest commander-in-chief of the Indian Army, wrote of the State Forces: 'There can be no question of their bravery, loyalty, patience in adversity and steadfastness under stress. They deserve to be remembered as such with honour.'

RANKS IN THE INDIAN ARMY

The Indian Army of the nineteenth and early twentieth centuries was unique in that it had two groups of officers – British and Indian. The ranks of the Indian officers and non-commissioned officers are shown below.

Cavalry	**Infantry**	**Rank insignia**	**British equivalent**
Risaldar Major	Subedar Major	Crown	
Risaldar*	Subedar	Two stars	
Jemadar	Jemadar	One star	
Kot Dafadar	Kot Havildar	Colour Sergeant	
Dafadar	Havildar	Three stripes	Sergeant
Lance Dafadar	Naik	Two stripes	Corporal
Acting Lance Dafadar	Lance Naik	One Stripe	Lance Corporal
Sowar	Sepoy	Trooper/Private	

One Indian officer usually served as assistant quartermaster and another as assistant adjutant; the latter was known as the woordy major. In the cavalry there was, for a period, the rank of ressaider, intermediate between the risaldar and the jemadar. In the State Forces, British officers were present only in an advisory capacity and therefore the senior ranks were also held by Indian officers as explained above.

Chapter 1

THE EARLY YEARS

Like so much else in Jodhpur, the credit for the inception of the Jodhpur Lancers rests with Sir Pratap Singh. In fact it wouldn't be wrong to say that the early history of this cavalry regiment is very closely linked to his.

Sir Pratap Singh – born 1845, an expert horseman and an enthusiastic sportsman who excelled in polo and pig-sticking by the age of nine – was regent for two years to the physically weak Maharaja Sir Sardar Singh, who died at the early age of thirty-one in 1911. The regency was extended to Sardar Singh's young son, Sumer Singh, who grew up to be a pleasure-loving young man. Sumer Singh died in 1918 when he was only twenty-one. Fortunately the new maharaja, Sir Umaid Singh, was to reign for twenty-nine years – the initial four years being under the regency of his grand-uncle Sir Pratap Singh.

Sir Pratap Singh might be said to be the father of modern Jodhpur; his statue is, to this day, venerated in the city. He was, in Philip Mason's words, 'every Englishman's idea of what an Indian prince should be – brave, courteous, dignified, handsome, manly' (Mason, 1974). When he first became regent the

Facing page: Sir Pratap Singh, who raised and trained the elite Jodhpur Lancers, photographed during Queen Victoria's golden jubilee in England in 1887.

state was in a perilous situation, especially with regard to its finances. He put Jodhpur on a much firmer footing, restructuring the administration, restoring law and order and allocating funds for irrigation and transport. In 1878 he attended the Delhi Durbar, where Queen Victoria, though not actually present, assumed the title of Empress of India. He was awarded the Empress of India Medal. In 1887 he paid his first visit to England when he was deputed by the viceroy marquis of Dufferin as the bearer of congratulations and good wishes of Jodhpur to Queen Victoria on her golden jubilee. He was gazetted as lieutenant colonel in 1887 in the British Army and placed on the staff of the queen, who was passionately interested in India and all things Indian; undoubtedly there was mutual admiration between the two. Sir Pratap returned to London in 1897 – his nephew by his side as his ADC – to participate in the procession to mark the queen's diamond jubilee.

Sir Pratap had every intention of creating a disciplined cavalry regiment of Jodhpur from the rather motley, untrained band of horsemen that existed then – the Jodhpur Lancers were raised in 1889 'discarding the age-old practice of the State army consisting of contingents provided by the Thakurs'.[1] He personally set about training his own retinue of about sixty troopers, teaching them riding himself while his private secretary, Raghubans Narayan, taught them the British system of drill. The Imperial Service Scheme was introduced in 1889. This is

Left: Maharaja Sumer Singh; Right: Maharaja Umaid Singh.
Facing page: Sir Pratap, Maharaja Sardar Singh and an officer.

when 1,200 sowars (riders) were enlisted in the two regiments of the Sardar Risala[2] – later referred to as the Jodhpur Lancers. The regimental barracks in Jodhpur consisted of small rooms with verandahs and the men's horses stood picketed in front of their quarters. The officers' mess was the first to be established by a State Forces unit. It is now a divisional headquarters officers' mess. According to Major Beatson, who assisted in training the new regiment: 'Sir Pratap spared no time, trouble or money in making the regiments as efficient as possible and the Rajputs followed his splendid example so that from the earliest days the discipline and tone of the regiments were all that could be desired.'

The Imperial State Forces Scheme was just the impetus that Sir Pratap needed to put the force on a more formal footing. He invited Colonel Prinsep, commandant of the 11th Bengal Lancers, and also Major Beatson of the same regiment to visit Jodhpur to advise him. Major Stuart Brownlow Beatson – son of Colonel Beatson, who had raised the Beatson's Horse in 1857 – was a most fortunate choice. He was to remain in Jodhpur for the first five years of the new regiment's operations. He also (perhaps equally importantly) introduced the modern version of polo to the state. He was first commissioned in 1873 into a British regiment, the 17th Foot, as was the custom at the time, before transferring to the 11th Bengal Lancers in 1876. Fluent in Persian and Pushtu, he was eventually to rise to become second-in-command of his regiment. He first saw active service on the North-West Frontier in 1878 when his services were brought to the notice of the headquarters of the Peshawar Division. He served in Afghanistan during the period 1878–80, in Egypt in 1882 and with the Malakand Field Force in 1897. This is when General Meiklejohn reported: 'Major SB Beatson commanded a squadron of the XI Bengal Lancers with great skill and

Major Stuart Beatson was invited to Jodhpur in 1890 to organize two cavalry regiments of the Imperial Service Troops.

Barracks for the Jodhpur lancers – Amongst the first buildings outside the walled city of Jodhpur.

dash.' After leaving Jodhpur Major Beatson attended Staff College and became military secretary and ADC to the commander-in-chief, Bengal. In 1900 he was appointed inspector general of Imperial Service Forces, retiring with the rank of major general. In 1903 he published *A History of the Imperial Service Troops of the Native States*.

Lord Roberts inspected the regiment in 1889 and wrote in the *Navy and Army Illustrated*: 'The gallant Rajput horsemen of Jodhpur had always been famous for their chivalrous bravery, unswerving fidelity and fearless self-devotion in their wars with the Marathas and the armies of the Moghul emperors, and I felt, as the superbly mounted squadrons passed before me, that they had lost none of their characteristics, and that blood and breeding must tell and would, if put to the test, achieve the same results now as of old.' He paid a second visit to Jodhpur in 1894 and inspected the Lancers together with the Bikaner Camel Corps. The viceroy, the marquis of Lansdowne, visited Jodhpur in 1890 and saw two squadrons of the regiment jumping walls and ditches, riding up and down steps and through a narrow passageway between high walls. He commented upon the extraordinary smartness of a magnificent body of troops which could only

Action at the Ratanada Palace Ground, Jodhpur at the turn of the century. Polo was the perfect training for war – a cavalry charge – and the Jodhpurs took to it like fish to water.

be explained by the fact that to both officers and men the service was a labour of love. 'Having seen the troops with my own eyes, and watched their soldierly bearing and movements, and their manner of riding, my satisfaction is complete.' He went on to add that should the government call upon the regiment for active service he was sure that they and Sir Pratap Singh 'will claim a place which will give them an opportunity of showing that the chivalrous traditions of the Rathore family have not been forgotten.' The chief inspecting officer, Colonel Mellis, reported that in no state had there been a greater spirit of enthusiasm than in Jodhpur. The legendary Rathore horsemanship meant that in 1893, only

The Jodhpur polo team, 1897. From left to right: Maharaj Zalim Singh, Dhokal Singh of Gorau, Major Stuart Beatson, Sir Pratap, and Hari Singh (Hurjee).

four years after the regiment's foundation, they won the Rajputana Challenge Cup and, captained by Sir Pratap, were amongst the finest teams ever seen. Polo was to be an important aspect of the regiment's activities down the years. In 1922, in the presence of the Prince of Wales, Jodhpur beat Patiala in the final to win the Prince of Wales Tournament. Even as late as in 1941, while waiting to be mechanized, the regiment would win the Inter-Regimental Championship.

The Jodhpur polo team, 1925. From left to right: Rao Raja Hanut Singh, Maharaja Umaid Singh, Thakur Prithi Singh Bera and Captain Bill Williams.

In 1892, some of the Jodhpur Lancers, together with Thakurs Hari Singh and Dhokal Singh, went to train with the 11th Bengal Lancers and joined them in the Black Mountain expedition on the North-West Frontier. This minor expedition was mounted because the Frontier tribes were harbouring a banished chief and refused either to expel or hand him over to the authorities. Sir Pratap was deeply disappointed that he could not take part in this first action undertaken by his

The Jodhpur Lancers performing Guard of Honour for Lord Curzon, viceroy of India, 1902.

regiment, especially as his request to act as an ADC to Lord Roberts (commander-in-chief, Indian Army) for the Afghan campaign of 1878 had also been denied. Sir Pratap was urged to be patient, was advised that his involvement in such petty affairs was not desirable, and was assured that he would not be forgotten when the chance arose to take part in a major campaign. In 1897, hardly had Sir Pratap returned from England when there were rumours once more of trouble on the North-West Frontier. This time his offer to serve *was* accepted and within nine hours of receiving orders he was on a special train heading for Peshawar. A report in the *Times* dated 14 September stated: 'Sir Partab Singh of Jodhpur has joined General Elles' staff at Shabkadr. His arrival has caused great enthusiasm among the native troops who are highly pleased that their own chief will personally take part in the campaign.' He was followed, a week later, by the whole of the regiment, which joined the Tirah Reserve Brigade at Rawalpindi. The Tirah Expedition was mounted as a show of strength in order to convince the tribes of the North-West Frontier – especially the Afridis and Orakzais – that the government would stand no nonsense and could move into and control their tribal areas whenever they wished to. The main body of the Jodhpurs unfortunately saw little fighting so there was no opportunity for them to earn distinction, though one field troop took part in the Mohmand expedition and two officers and fifty-three dafadars and sowars of the Lancers were employed as convoy escorts and on a couple of occasions were engaged by the enemy. The regimental history of the 11th Bengal Lancers, coincidentally written by Captain (later Lieutenant Colonel) Eustace Maxwell, who served with the Jodhpur Lancers in 1914, records the arrival of

The Lancers on parade during the viceroy Lord Minto's visit to Jodhpur, 1908.

a troop of Jodhpur Lancers which was attached to the 11th Lancers and served with them for a month. Sir Pratap and the troop officers lived in the regular officers' mess when they were with the regiment. At this time the 11th Lancers were commanded by Major Beatson, who had the honour of being appointed a Companion of the Bath during the campaign.

Sir Pratap sustained a minor wound and was mentioned in despatches on three occasions. General Lockhart's despatch, reprinted in the *Times* dated 18 April 1898, read: 'I take the opportunity of expressing my thanks to Lt Col HH the Maharaj Dhiraj Sir Partab Singh who was attached to me throughout the campaign as extra ADC. This very gallant Rajput nobleman was wounded on 29 November and characteristically concealed the fact until I discovered it by accident some days after the occurrence.' Apparently the game was given away when General Lockhart's nephew went to shake hands with Sir Pratap and Hari Singh cried out, 'Take care, his hand is wounded!' Queen Victoria wrote expressing her concern, and General Lockhart's reply to Her Majesty's enquiry is preserved in the Royal Archives at Windsor: 'Maharaj Sir Pratab Singh is deeply grateful for Her Majesty's gracious enquiries. His wound was slight and he has now recovered but he had a narrow escape.' Major General Elles, commanding the Field Force, wrote: 'The Imperial Service troops under my command proved their fitness to fight in the first line and were treated exactly the same as regular Indian troops. The cavalry escorts of the Jodhpur cavalry did good reconnaissance work on more than one occasion.' Brigadier General Lockhart too gave his opinion: 'I consider the Jodhpur Lancers to be a first-class

Imperial Service Troops await the arrival of the viceroy, 1916.

regiment; its arrangements were excellent, and every one of the men gave proof of smartness as a soldier. I believe that the days that they spent out of their own country provided them with an excellent opportunity for training.' The adjutant general in India wrote to the military secretary of the Government of India: 'The Imperial Service troops attached to the Field force have taken their full share in the hardships of the campaign and, fighting side by side with their comrades in

the regular army, have given tangible proof of their readiness and that of their rulers to assist in the defence of the Empire.' This letter, dated 24 February 1898, was published in the *Gazette of India* later that year. At the conclusion of the campaign, Sir Pratap was promoted to full colonel and awarded the Order of the Bath; the troops involved were eligible for the India Medal (1895–1902) with the clasp 'Tirah 1897–98'.

Chapter 2

THE JODHPURS IN CHINA

During the second half of the nineteenth century, European countries were keen to develop stronger commercial links with China, especially in the profitable opium trade. From time to time open war broke out, forcing the Chinese to grant concessions which included the establishment of trading posts along the coast – the British at Wei-Hai-Wei, the French at Kwangchowan and the Germans at Kiaochow. The traders were followed by missionaries, who wished to convert the Chinese to Christianity. The latter responded to what they quite reasonably saw as an invasion of their homeland, through a number of secret societies. Prominent amongst these were the Boxers, whose slogan was 'Destroy the Foreigner!' The Boxers were secretly supported by the Dowager Empress, Tzu Hsi.

By the year 1900 the Boxers were out of control; Chinese Christians were massacred, missionaries tortured and killed, a railway station destroyed. In June, now supported by regular Chinese troops, they set fire to a large area of the capital, Peking. On 20 June, they surrounded the Legation Quarter of the city where the foreign embassies were concentrated. The countries whose legations were besieged responded by assembling the first truly multinational force in

Facing page: Sir Pratap Singh.

The Lancers in the bitter cold of Shan Hai Kuan, China. Back row from left: Bukhtawar Singh, Hari Singh, Sir Pratap, Major Turner, a Japanese soldier, Akai Singh. Front row: Amar Singh, Captain Pinchard, Captain Hughes, Captain Alexander, the captain's dog.

history, comprising troops from France, Germany, Great Britain, India, Japan, Russia and the United States of America. The Indian contingent included State Forces from Alwar, Bikaner, Jodhpur and Malerkotla, and were accompanied by the Maharajas of Bikaner and Jodhpur. However, the siege was lifted in mid-August before many of the Indian troops arrived. It was not until 6 August that the 4th Indian Infantry Brigade, which included dismounted men of the Bikaner Camel Corps as well as the Jodhpur Lancers, was ordered to leave for China.

Amar Singh, a protégé of Sir Pratap, was a risaldar in the Jodhpur Lancers at that time and wrote a daily diary that gives us a first-hand account of the exploits of the regiment in China. He acted as regimental adjutant and secretary to Sir Pratap throughout the campaign. Sir Pratap was, of course, overjoyed at

Three squadrons of the Jodhpur Lancers on parade in Shan Hai Kuan, China, 1901.

the news that the regiment had been selected for service overseas, with him as honorary commandant. Hari (Hurjee) Singh, a favourite of Sir Pratap's, was the commanding officer. Major Turner, a squadron commander in Gardner's Horse and the senior British adviser to Imperial Service troops in Rajasthan, together with Captain E.M. Hewiss, also accompanied the regiment to China. When the orders to move were received the regiment was quartered at Mathura in United Provinces because of shortage of fodder in Jodhpur. They had relieved the 9th Lancers, who had been sent to South Africa to join other British troops who were fighting the Boers. From Mathura the regiment went by special trains to Calcutta, where they embarked for China at the end of August, regimental headquarters being on board the *SS Mohawk.* After thirty days at sea, during which time the regiment lost six horses, the Lancers arrived at Shanghai on 24

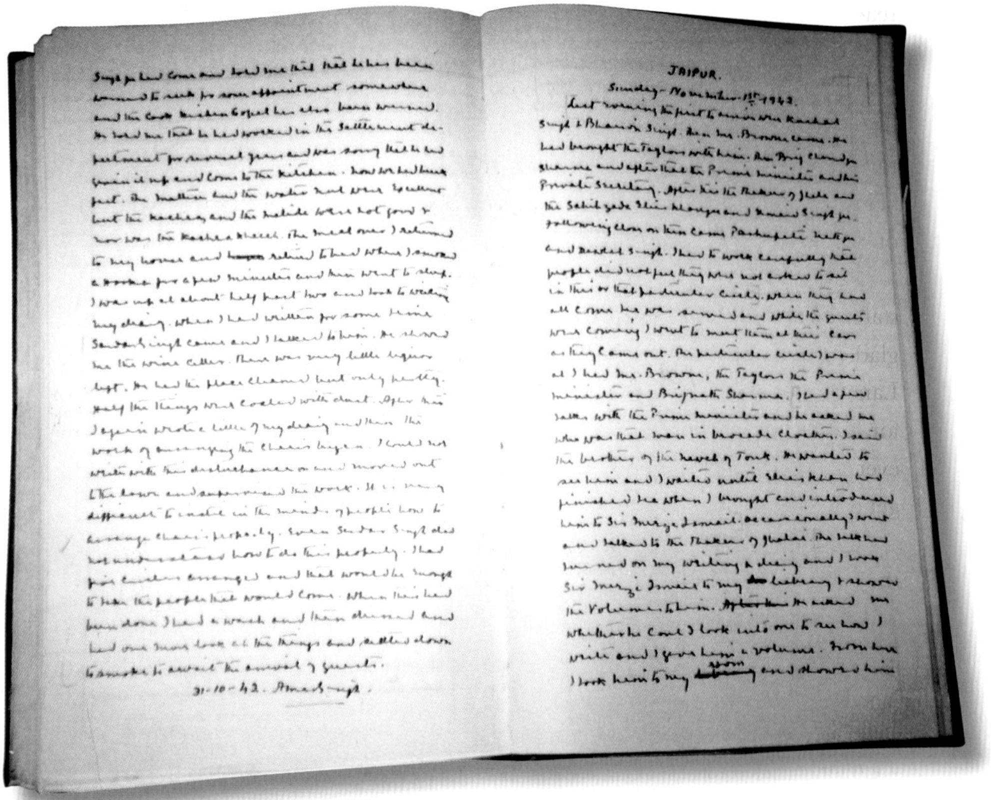

Pages from Amar Singh's diary.

September, and, having disembarked, waited there for a fortnight before they were assigned a task.

Sections of the regiment took part in the Nikko Shimanzai and Funnig expeditions, where they saw some fighting. At one time, the regiment was divided into fifteen detachments. Some of these were guarding the railway to Peking while others were sixty miles from it! On 8 October, Amar Singh and his squadron were ordered to take part in a reconnaissance sweep around Shanghai. The squadron was divided into four patrols, Amar Singh accompanying one of them under the command of Jemadar Bhaboot Singh with twenty sowars that were to ride out as far as Wusung, about ten miles away. When the patrol reached the village of Wusung, Amar Singh sent back the following report: 'Way is all clear. No signs of hostility appear at all.... Country all flat but full of canals and ditches.... Horses take to the stone bridges quite willingly. In some places the path lies alongside the line of houses'. The patrol proceeded on to the railway station, from where Amar Singh sent a further report, before returning. (This report commented on the rain, which made the ground slippery, and also on the number of ditches and buildings that made the area difficult for cavalry.)

Amar Singh's reports were duly forwarded to the Brigade headquarters, and a staff officer – Captain Stewart – replied to Major Turner: 'The General would be glad if you would express to Sir Pratap his appreciation of the way the Jodhpur Lancers worked today. He is afraid they must have had a very long and trying day for both men and horses. The country he knew was a very bad one but he had every confidence, which has not been misplaced, that the Jodhpur cavalry would get over it if anyone could.'

On 9 October, the *Mohawk* sailed to Shan Hai Kuan, northeast of Peking at the eastern end of the Great Wall of China and strategically sited on the coast

Sir Pratap Singh and his staff in their stables in Shan Hai Kuan, China, 1900–01.

road to Manchuria. Here the Lancers were to remain throughout the long cold winter. On the night of 31 January 1901 there was thirty-nine degrees of frost; the ink froze in the ink stands. Amar Singh commented in his diary that the city was dirty, filthy and very smelly but that the regiment's quarters were good, with warm stables for the horses. The troops settled down to a routine of patrols searching for weapons in the surrounding villages. On Christmas Day there was a gymkhana organized by the allied forces. The staff section of the Jodhpur Lancers won the tent-pegging competition and Amar Singh himself won a race which involved pistol-shooting and riding. Major Turner presented him with a silver bottle and two tumblers as a prize. Colonel Beatson wrote: 'The officers and men had a full share of roughing it but they were always willing, ready for anything and absolutely uncomplaining. All showed great hardiness and withstood the privation and intense cold exceedingly well. The presence of Sir Pratap was a great incentive to all ranks by the splendid example he set, making nothing of the hardest work and privations in the severest weather.'

The regiment's only serious engagement with the enemy came on 12 January 1901 when shots were fired at a Jodhpur party, which was out collecting wood by a large body of Chinese armed brigands, about five miles north-east of Shan Hai Kuan. Some mules were hit and the men scattered. Three men entered a house in the nearby village of Lamasu but nine others under Dafadar Dool Singh climbed a small rise and opened fire upon the enemy, while Sowar Sheoram Singh rode back to the camp to raise alarm. One of the men in the house was mortally wounded and the Chinese set fire to the roof. However, when the two Lancers who had not been wounded were driven out by the heat and smoke, they found that the relief party under Captain Pinchard had already arrived and driven off the enemy.

As the Lancers rode further on, a Chinese man armed with a rifle was spotted in a ditch. The colonel and another officer, together with Sheoram Singh, went forward in an attempt to capture him alive. However, a bullet from the Chinese man badly wounded Sheoram Singh, who died shortly afterwards. Amar Singh was leading his troop at a brisk trot when they saw about twenty armed Chinese ahead of them making for the village of Lijapoo. He persuaded Major Turner to charge the enemy but the sowars were scattered and it proved impossible to form a proper line for the charge. However, Amar Singh struck three men with his lance and wounded two more with his revolver. By this time the Lancers were under heavy fire from about 100 men in the village, so they fell back. In this skirmish, two Lancers as well as six of the Chinese brigands were killed. Amar Singh received a bullet through his coat.

Dafadar Dool Singh was awarded the Indian Order of Merit, the highest decoration available to an Indian soldier before they became eligible for the Victoria Cross in 1911. It is said that, in keeping with the correct pig-sticking etiquette, a senior is allowed the first kill. The Lancers therefore refused to use the points of their lances at first, shouting 'Has Sirkar (Sir Pratap) killed yet?' Unfortunately for the story, Amar Singh reports in his diary that Sir Pratap was not actually present at this engagement at Lijapoo.

On 27 February, General Richardson, commanding the Cavalry Brigade, inspected the regiment in its quarters and was very pleased with what he found. His report, written on 1 March, reads as follows:

'Drill and Manoeuvre: Three squadrons paraded for my inspection. The regiment was drilled by the commanding officer and the squadron commanders. The pace was smooth and steady, the direction and distance carefully maintained. Dismounted practice was well and intelligently performed...

Equitation: The riding was good. The men sit still and are evidently well instructed...

Equipment: Is mostly English manufacture, carefully cleaned and looked after.

Discipline: Is well-maintained, conduct good.... The Jodhpur Lancers are a very fine regiment of Imperial Service troops, fit for service in every respect.'

As military action in China drew to a close, Sir Pratap and his staff went to Peking before going on to visit Japan. At Peking, horse races and an assault-at-arms were arranged for the Allied Expeditionary Force and Amar Singh won the steeplechase. At the gymkhana the Lancers won eleven first prizes while their great rivals, the Cossacks, won only two! A trophy from this event is preserved at Narain Niwas, the home which Amar Singh built for himself in Jaipur and which is now a hotel. The regiment returned to Calcutta in July 1901, having established a fine reputation for itself in China. Major General Reid, commanding the 3rd Brigade of the British Contingent, wrote of the Lancers: 'A very fine regiment,

Chinese cannon trophies captured by the Jodhpur Lancers in 1901.

animated by a very fine spirit and Sir Pratab is the beau ideal of a native prince. The Lancers were largely represented in the expedition to the Laushan Hills and Chimunsai and a field troop behaved very well when engaged with marauders outside the great wall last January. The regiment is thoroughly efficient and fit for service.' A general order of 1903 ordered that: 'In commemoration of their gallant conduct and distinguished services during the operations in China in 1900, "China 1900" should be borne upon the Lancer's colours and appointments.' Those Lancers who went to China were awarded the campaign medal with its crimson ribbon edged yellow.

Amar Singh was most concerned about the discrimination shown by the British towards the Indian troops. For instance, British soldiers were not expected to salute Indian officers – not even Sir Pratap. In his opinion the Lancers had done good work, had lived up to every expectation others had of them, and had borne the hardships of winter most admirably. He believed that the regiment was better than any of the cavalry he had seen in China; the men being more skilful horsemen with higher quality horses. In 1902 he joined the Imperial

The maharaja gifted the Chinese cannon trophies to the police headquarters, Jodhpur.

Cadet Corps, which was founded in that year, and of which Sir Pratap was honorary commandant. Maharaja Sardar Singh joined at the same time but left after four terms.

We shall meet Amar Singh again later in our story.

The Imperial Cadet corps was founded by Lord Curzon, the then viceroy, with the aim of providing a military education to high-class Indians and to transform them into 'officers and gentlemen,' able to serve alongside British officers. Curzon was keen to encourage suitable young men to join the Indian Army or, at least, to become officers in their own State Forces; entry was restricted to the sons of princes and nobles. The first batch of twenty-one cadets included four maharajas and two heirs apparent, the remainder generally being noblemen or the sons of noblemen who had attended one of the four Chiefs' Colleges at Ajmer, Lahore, Rajkot and Indore. The cadets spent half the year at Meerut and the remainder at Dehra Dun. The preliminary course lasted two years. Those who wished to seriously pursue a military career would then undergo a more sustained military education lasting another year and a half, similar to the course at Sandhurst.

Viceroy Lord Curzon inspecting the Imperial Cadets, 1905.

During the thirteen years of the Corps' existence, nearly eighty cadets passed through the unit.

Sir Pratap had very strong views about the nature of the training that the Corps should provide. 'It should furnish whole-time occupation for the young princes. In addition to brain work, physical work should also be taken from them, that they may go to bed fatigued and get sound sleep. As the Cadet Corps is a military school for these young men, care should be taken from the beginning to create in them a taste for enduring hardships.' One imagines that Sir Pratap applied exactly the same principles to the training of the Jodhpur Lancers. However, he may not have seen the need for the higher and more technical aspects of the education provided by the Corps. For Sir Pratap 'A steed, a steed of matchless speed, a sword of metal keen' – with the sword being wielded by a gallant Rathore – represented the acme of military perfection. In 1902 Sir Pratap was appointed Maharaja of Idar, a small state in Gujarat, by Lord Curzon. He took with him six dafadars of the Jodhpur Lancers, whom he promoted to the rank of jemadar. Two officers of the Jodhpur Lancers also accompanied him – Bukhtawar Singh, who was appointed military secretary, and his brother Kishore Singh, who became superintendent of police. Bukhtawar Singh had served on Sir Pratap's staff in China and had been adjutant of the Jodhpur Lancers.

The two Imperial Durbars held in Delhi in 1903 and 1911 mark the apogee of the British Raj in India. Harking back to the magnificence of the Mughals, they were designed to over-awe with an impression of the might of the British Empire. In addition, they were an opportunity to reward those Indian rulers who were loyal to the British cause. Vast tented camps were laid out for the princely rulers on a site north of the city and the chiefs vied with one another in as far as the opulence of their pavilions was concerned. So large was the site that a narrow-gauge railway, seven miles in length, was laid out. There was a dairy as well as a post and telegraph office in the camp.

The Coronation Durbar in 1903 was a splendid affair organized by the viceroy, Lord Curzon. For their entry into Delhi, the viceroy and Lady Curzon, followed by the Duke and Duchess of Connaught, rode on two elephants at the head of two columns of magnificently arrayed elephants, 166 in all, each bearing a ruling chief. Leading the columns were the two most senior chiefs – the Nizam of Hyderabad and the Maharaja of Mysore – on their elephants. The Imperial Cadet Corps acted as personal bodyguard to the viceroy. With Sir Pratap as their honorary commandant, the cadets included Maharaja Sardar Singh of Jodhpur and Kanwar Amar Singh of Kanota. Dressed in white uniforms with sky-blue facings laced with gold and mounted on black chargers, they attracted much attention. The Jodhpur Lancers under their commandant, Thakur Jas Singh, took part in the manoeuvres held in November and December 1902 and directed

HH Maharaja Sardar Singh in the uniform of the Jodhpur Lancers. Sir Pratap raised the regiment in his name – Sardar Risala – when he was the crown prince.

by Lord Kitchener. They then paraded in the great review held on 8 January 1903 as part of the Durbar celebrations, together with detachments from Alwar, Bhopal, Gwalior, Hyderabad, Mysore, Patiala and Rampur. They were to have been led by the maharaja on this occasion but unfortunately he was indisposed. Sir Pratap, now a major general, had been decorated with the GCSI by Queen Victoria. While he was in London in 1903 prior to the Durbar, he was promoted to field marshal and made a knight commander of the Order of the Bath in recognition of his services in China. Jas Singh's appointment was announced in the Durbar Honours list. In the International Polo Cup, played as part of the festivities, a team from Jodhpur was beaten in the final by a team from Alwar, a game in which both the respective maharajas played.

Sir Pratap was also present as commandant of the Imperial Cadet Corps at the great Delhi Durbar of 1911 at which King George V and Queen Mary held court. The crowds were disappointed because the King-Emperor made his entry into Delhi on a horse rather than the traditional elephant. Amar Singh, who as a member of the Corps had attended the 1903 Durbar, rejoined his old unit for the occasion, borrowing his brother's uniform. The Jodhpur Lancers, together with lancers from Hyderabad, Kashmir and Mysore, formed the 2nd Cavalry Brigade. The sixteen-year-old Maharaja Sumer Singh, who was studying at Wellington College in England, returned home for the event. Riding a white horse and wearing his white and gold uniform, he received a loud welcome from the crowds lining the route of the procession. The brigade trotted past the saluting base to the tune of 'The Garb of Old Gaul', which may seem a rather strange choice of music, being the regimental march of the Scots Guards. During the investiture the maharaja acted as a page to the king while Maharaj Sher Singh, commandant of the 2nd Sardar Risala, was an honorary ADC to the viceroy. Sir Pratap was decorated with the Grand Cross of the Royal Victorian Order, a decoration within the personal gift of the sovereign. Somewhat surprisingly, the Lancers did not field a team in the polo tournament this year but Lieutenant Harnat Singh, riding a regimental horse, was second in the race for Imperial Service troops for the King Emperor's Cup. It was at this Durbar that George V declared that henceforth Delhi would become the capital of India.

Chapter 3

FRANCE 1914-18

The assassination of the Austrian Archduke Ferdinand in Sarajevo in 1914 set off a chain reaction as the European nations honoured their mutual treaty obligations and declared war on one another. Germany, faced with a war on two fronts, planned to hold off the numerically stronger Russian army in the East while gaining a swift victory against the French in the West. The Schlieffen plan, developed and refined by the German General Staff during the years preceding the war, envisaged seven huge German armies sweeping through northern France and Belgium, and enveloping Paris.

The violation of Belgian neutrality brought Great Britain into the war and the British Expeditionary Force (BEF), consisting initially of a mere four divisions and a cavalry brigade (the German Kaiser referred to it as a 'Contemptible little Army') was sent to France. Crossing the frontier into Belgium, the BEF held off the German forces opposed to them at their opening engagements at Mons and Le Cateau. However, the British were compelled to fall back in order to align themselves with the French troops.

Facing page: France 1914: Sir Pratap with General Joffre, commander-in-chief of French forces on the Western Front, and General Haig, commander of the British Expeditionary Force during the First World War.

Sir Pratap (left), General Rimington (centre) and the Maharaja of Ratlam (right) at the Western Front.

The French and British allies managed to hold the German advance on the line of the River Marne and then to push them back to the River Aisne, where the latter dug in on the northern bank on the higher ground. Then began what was known as 'The Race to the Sea' as the Germans and the Allied armies each tried to outflank the other and to swing around behind the open flank. The period of mobile warfare ended with a continuous line of trenches which stretched from the North Sea to the neutral Swiss border. The small Belgian Army was next to the North Sea and the BEF (now reinforced to a strength of six infantry divisions and two cavalry divisions) was centred around the Belgian town of Ypres on the left flank of the French Army. At the start of the war, Indian troops had been the only reinforcements available to the British in large numbers as the armed forces from Australia, Canada, New Zealand and South Africa – though so important later in the war – were at this stage very small in terms of their numbers. It was decided that an Indian corps, consisting of the Lahore and Meerut infantry divisions, together with the Secunderabad Cavalry Brigade, be sent to France; the first troops landed at Marseille on 26 September 1914.

When the war broke out, Sir Pratap had immediately telegraphed King George V, offering his services. 'I will deem it a special mark of royal favour and a great honour if allowed to serve on Your Majesty's staff,' he wrote. He placed all the resources of the state, including the Jodhpur Lancers, at the disposal of the king. At the age of sixty-nine, he told Sir Harry Watson – the inspector general of Imperial Service Troops – that he wanted to lead his regiment in a charge and to die at the head of his men. Sir Harry, with what turned out to be remarkable foresight, said that there would be no opportunity for cavalry charges in France, to which Sir Pratap replied that he would create an opportunity. In addition to the Jodhpur Lancers, troops from twelve other states took part in the Great War.

Unfortunately, the Indian soldiers who landed in France in 1914 had not been trained nor were they equipped to fight a highly trained and well-equipped European army. Many of the troops arrived without adequate clothing to withstand a harsh European winter. The sepoys were given more modern rifles when they landed in Marseille but had little opportunity to practise their use before they were thrust piecemeal into what later came to be known as the First Battle of Ypres. The cavalry were issued bayonets, which they had never used and which did not fit their rifles. The Indians had no corps artillery and were

India's contribution to the First World War was immense in terms of manpower (combatant and non-combatant), supplies, animals and monetary support to the Empire. The Jodhpur Lancers were one of the first to arrive in Europe in 1914.

understrength compared to a British corps. However, the BEF had suffered very heavy casualties in the opening battles of the war and the Indian infantry were thrust hurriedly into the trenches at the end of October in order to meet the heavy German attacks in Ypres. Ultimately the Germans failed to break through but, to use the Duke of Wellington's phrase, 'It was a near run thing'.

The following year, in March 1915, the two Indian infantry divisions attacked with some success at Neuve-Chapelle; the cavalry was held ready to exploit the breakthrough which never came because the attack stalled. This was the first of a number of such disappointments which were to follow. In July, the cavalrymen went into the trenches to relieve the British infantry, who were preparing for the Battle of Loos. Just before the attack the cavalry was withdrawn into reserve but once again the hopes of a decisive breakthrough and subsequent cavalry exploitation were dashed. At the end of the year the Indian infantry, having suffered heavy casualties, left France and the cavalry were reorganized into two divisions. Some regiments returned to India while others were sent to Mesopotamia, leaving only ten Indian cavalry regiments (including the Jodhpur Lancers) in France. At the opening of the Battle of the Somme in 1916 it was reported (incorrectly) that the cavalry had broken through the German lines. Lord Esher wrote to Lord Stamfordham from Paris: 'Sir Pratab was here for the Review which bored him to death. When I told him that the cavalry had gone through, he nearly had a fit. He rushed back to them at the earliest possible moment, fearing that he was going to lose the chance for which he had waited so long.'

From the two regiments of the Jodhpur Imperial Service Lancers, one composite and complete regiment was mobilized during the second week of April 1914. Majors H.H. Holden (5th Cavalry) and A.D. Strong (10th Lancers), and Capt E.L. Maxwell (11th Lancers) accompanied the regiment as Special Service officers. A total of twenty-eight Indian officers, 497 NCOs and troopers, and fifty-eight followers left for France. The 'followers' were unique to the Indian Army. They included the cooks, grooms (syces) and water carriers (*bhistis*). A *bhisti* was made famous in Kipling's well-known poem 'Gunga Din'. Sadly many followers did not return to India. A squadron of Alwar Imperial Service Lancers (five officers, 142 rank and file and sixteen followers) was attached to the regiment as a 10 per cent reinforcement. Major General Sir Pratap Singh, regent of Marwar, and the sixteen-year-old ruler of Marwar, Maharaja Sumer Singh, accompanied the regiment which was under the command of Colonel Maharaj Sher Singhji. Captain Maxwell wrote to his brother in August: 'The young Maharaja has beautiful manners and a nice fresh way with him. The Commanding Officer (CO), Maharaja Sumer Singh, is a very smart-looking fellow. A good number of the officers speak English. The men look excellent and probably are, as the Rajputs are one of the great traditional fighting races, but the horses are mostly small Arab ponies, many of them long past the age at which a horse by regulation should be cast (i.e., retired) from the service.'

The Lancers had left Jodhpur on 29 August 1914 bound for the Middle East, where it was intended that they guard the Suez Canal. However, Sir Pratap had telegraphed the king before leaving Bombay, requesting that the Lancers be sent to France and not to any lesser theatre of war. So, thanks to Sir Pratap's intervention, the Jodhpur Lancers became the only Imperial Service cavalry

Left to right: The Maharaja of Ratlam, Sir Pratap and his son Hanut Singh in France.

regiment to serve in France. They sailed from Bombay on 20 September, with two squadrons and the Headquarters embarked on the *SS City of Birmingham* and the other two squadrons on the *SS Tactician*. They disembarked at Marseilles on 12 October, and travelled by train to the depot at Orleans, where they drew coats, warm underclothing and bayonets. They were brigaded together with the Deccan Horse and the Poona Horse of the Secunderabad Cavalry Brigade. This brigade eventually became part of the 2nd Indian Cavalry Division, which in turn was later designated as the 5th Cavalry Division. In 1917, the Jodhpur Lancers were transferred to the Lucknow Cavalry Brigade.

The Lancers recieved their first exposure to 'modern warfare' on 5 November 1914 when 100 troopers dug trenches behind the front line between Laventie and Neuve-Chapelle from 9.00 a.m. until 4.00 p.m., behind a covering party of fifty men. This digging continued for several days, interrupted on 9 November when two regiments of the Secunderabad Cavalry Brigade were hurriedly moved forward to meet a German attack while the Jodhpur Lancers remained in reserve. Sir Pratap wrote of this period: 'Though we were just in the rear of the fighting line, the sounds of guns and volleys of musketry were so tremendous that sometimes we were unable to hear each other. We had orders always to be ready, and therefore had to keep our men armed and the horses always saddled.'

On 11 November the working party in the trenches was severely shelled. Spy mania was at its height at this time. The War Diary suggests that this was as a result of the activity of German spies, which seems most unlikely.

Men of the regiment were inspected by the much-loved former commander-in-chief of the Indian Army – Field-Marshal Lord Roberts – a few days before he died on 14 November. Two representatives from the regiment joined the Guard of Honour while the body of Lord Roberts lay in Rouen Cathedral. Sir Pratap accompanied the body back to England and attended the funeral. Sir John Wilcox, who commanded the Indian Corps, together with Prince Arthur of Connaught, visited the regiment on 19 November, and two squadrons were inspected by the Prince of Wales and General Wilcox on 21 November.

On 23 November, fifty men under Major Strong went into the trenches to act as a reserve; five days later a slightly smaller group with Captain Maxwell joined the Poona Horse in the firing line around Festubert. The conditions facing the Jodhpur Lancers here were far removed from the hot and dusty plains of Rajasthan. The trenches at this stage of the war were makeshift and quite unlike the more carefully constructed trenches of later years. Also, in this area of Flanders, the water table was very high and the trenches tended to flood. As recorded in the regimental history of the Poona Horse: 'The trenches were in a very bad state, half full of water, and many men had to stand in them up to their thighs throughout the night; the cold was intense.' During their stay in the front line – despite the fact that the Germans were so close they could throw hand-grenades across – only two Lancers were wounded. On 27 November, Captain Maxwell wrote: 'A party of the regiment is now in the front line under Strong, and in an hour's time I am going to take 36 lances, or rather rifles, to reinforce the Poona Horse who have a squadron or more in the trenches. It is a life of ceaseless strain, always waiting for something which may or may not happen.' A few days later he wrote: 'They are the worst trenches that I have ever seen and are not

King Albert of Belgium with King George V of Great Britain and Northern Ireland in Belgium, accompanied by Sir Pratap Singh (centre), the Prince of Wales and Maharaja Ganga Singh of Bikaner (extreme right).

HERBERG
BOND DER GEWEZEN SOLDATEN

really fit to be held. The men of the regiment are certainly in astonishing good health, their only disability arising from feet swollen by the recent cold, and so painful as to make their owners useless for any work on foot.' During this period the commanding officer, Maharaj Sher Singh, and Major Holden, together with fifty men of the regiment, were taken out of the trenches and inspected by the King-Emperor George V. The maharaja and Sir Pratap met King Albert of the Belgians; Monsieur Poincare, the president of the French Republic; and Marshal Joffre, commander-in-chief of the French Army. A photograph shows Sir Pratap talking with Joffre and Sir Douglas Haig, commander of the BEF.

The conditions in the trenches were appalling, but the soldiers seemed to have fared relatively well when out of the front line. A soldier of the Hodson's Horse wrote home to India in 1916 as follows: 'I am most comfortable. We live nowadays in the houses of the French people and they look after us better even than their own parents. They are ready to give us coffee, milk or hot water at any hour. They are so kind that they even kill our vermin for us. (Presumably the lice in their clothes.) The French ladies look upon it as their duty to wake us in the morning and to give us tea and toast and to bring us hot water, soap and towels. The government too has been most thoughtful for us. We get warm clothing, tea, ghee, meat, spices, cigarettes, everything we want.' Similarly a trooper from the Poona Horse wrote: 'Food and warm clothing, pay and allowances are on a scale that has never been heard of before. We get every kind of sweetmeats and fruit, milk and tobacco.'[1] The Indian troops, perhaps because many of them came from a farming background, were well-liked by the French peasants.

A Jodhpur Lancer wrote home, possibly to his father: 'When you wrote to me some little while back you told me to serve the government faithfully as my ancestors had done. This indeed is the very first principle of our clan and for this reason it is a matter of the greatest pride to us that the Chief of our clan, Maharaja Sir Pratap Singh himself, though he is over seventy-two years of age, was not backward in serving the King.' Indian officers were sent on leave to London, where they were feted and often received their gallantry medals from the king-emperor himself. Risaldar Mohammed Ikram Khan of the Hodson's Horse wrote home to India: 'I went to London to have an interview with His Majesty The King. The King spoke to me in his own auspicious tongue. I am profoundly grateful to His Majesty for his kind treatment of us and am always

A group of Jodhpur Lancer officers and NCOs in France. Major Thakur Dalpat Singh standing behind (left) of Sir Pratap (seated fourth from left in middle row). His sons Kanwar Sagat Singh and Kanwar Hanut Singh in the first row.

praying that God in justice will grant him the victory.' An Indian officer who had been wounded and who was in hospital wrote home: 'The men and women in England are extremely fond of Indians. Whenever I go for a walk, all these people recognize an Indian officer and they are delighted when he speaks to them in English. They take us to their homes and entertain us kindly.' Ten officers from the Jodhpur Lancers went on leave to England in February 1917.

The Lancers were in reserve during the first part of December and 200 men went back into the trenches on 19 December. On 21 December these men, under the command of Colonel Thakur Pratap Singh (not to be confused with Sir Pratap Singh) and accompanied by Major Strong, took part in a dismounted attack by the Secunderabad Cavalry Brigade at Givenchy, forming the second line alongside the Deccan Horse. There was no preliminary reconnaissance,

The arrival of Indian troops in Europe was met with great interest amongst the local population. Indian soldiers got along well with the civilian population of France and Belgium, at times forming relationships that outlived the war.

the exact position of the enemy was unknown, and heavy rain meant that the men were standing in water for an hour before the attack was made at 4.30 a.m. Not surprisingly in these conditions, the attack failed to reach its objective. In this action Major Strong and Jemadar Guman Singh were both wounded, Dafadar Khet Singh and Sowars Gulab Singh and Sardar Singh were killed and six troopers were wounded, one of whom (Sowar Khim Singh) later died of his wounds. The remnants of the Cavalry Brigade reformed and reorganized, ready to meet the next German attack. The whole of the Indian Corps was relieved on the evening of 22 December. When the regiment withdrew from the line, five Indian officers were suffering from frozen feet. Some months later Amar Singh wrote of these events in his diary: 'I think that this taking and retaking of trenches went on for about three days and there was terrible slaughter.... The first day when the fighting was severest there were all sorts of reinforcements and a great deal of cavalry, among them some Jodhpur Lancers. There never was

The Jodhpur Lancers in France with children of the local village, where they were stationed.

such confusion as on the night of the first day. People were launched into attack but were given no objective. There were no orders. The consequence was that nothing important was done.'

After Amar Singh and his brigade left Orleans, they moved nearer the front line and Brigade headquarters were established in the village of Les Lobes. Some of their transport got stuck in the mud – a foretaste of things to come. Amar Singh kept in close touch with his old comrades, visiting the regiment again on 10 December at Busnes. On 17 December he wrote in his diary: 'The trenches were about three feet in liquid mud.' And on 22 December: 'I hear that there was quite a heavy casualty list among the Jodhpur Lancers.' On 27 December he went to see them again, this time at the Chateau of Longheim. The regiment was billeted in the village of Witternesse for the rest of the winter. This typical French village has changed little in the last ninety years and today it is easy to imagine the Lancers billeted with their horses in the farm buildings which line the main street and walking down to the mill in the centre of the village – perhaps even fishing in the mill-stream. Though the ground was too wet and muddy to allow mounted exercise the men and horses kept fit by route marches along the roads and were trained in the use of their newly issued bayonets. Captain Maxwell wrote in December: 'I wondered if they (the Germans) knew that for several hundred yards the trenches were held by Indian cavalry quite untrained to trench work and not skilled in the use of the bayonet. I am sure our fellows would have done very well had they been trained, but they are very much handicapped by the circumstances and hardly have a fair chance.' In November 1915 Captain Maxwell was transferred to the 19th Battalion of the Durham Light Infantry. Later he commanded the 23rd Battalion of the Manchester Regiment and was killed on 20 July 1916.

In January 1915 the regiment was first inspected by Field Marshal Sir John French, commanding the British forces in France, and later by the Prince of Wales. On these occasions the bearer section of Number 132 Indian (Jodhpur) Cavalry Field Ambulance paraded with the regiment, with Lancers acting as drivers for the ambulances. This unit supported the Lancers throughout their time in France. Apart from minor wounds and ailments, there were cases of pneumonia and bronchitis, which took a steady toll on the regiment. In spring the regiment undertook a variety of training, practising outposts, defending a position, a new method of dismounted attack and attack at night. Maharaja Sumer Singh and Sir Pratap were mentioned in despatches. On 11 March the regiment moved forward to Burbure, anticipating a breakthrough following the Indian Corps attack at Neuve-Chapelle, but were back at Witternesse on the 14th. Frequently during May the regiment was at very short notice to move either to exploit a breakthrough or to repel a German counterattack. Visits by George V, Queen Mary and the Prince of Wales to France were much appreciated by the troops. Major Dalpat Singh wrote to a friend in Idar State: 'I am very happy here on the battlefield. The Generals gave a big luncheon to all the Indian officers in which I took part. Our King and Queen came here. The King visited the Army in every place and shells fell quite near him. The Queen did a round of all the hospitals.'

During the greater part of 1915 the regiment spent most of its time training, wiring, laying light railways and preparing a track for cavalry advance. In July a working party was shelled while passing through the village of Les Brebis;

A troop of Jodhpur Lancers form a firing line at Linghem, France.

Dafadars Daula Singh and Nahar Singh were killed and Risaldar Guman Singh and Dafadar Khuman Singh wounded. In the same month, Captain Thakur Ragunath Singh, who was acting as ADC to the Raja of Ratlam at Brigade headquarters, died of pneumonia and was buried at Boulogne. In August the regiment moved south, a journey of over sixty miles, and bivouacked in water meadows at Flixecourt on the banks of the Somme Canal, where they were taught bomb-throwing. Major Strong, having recovered from his wound, rejoined the

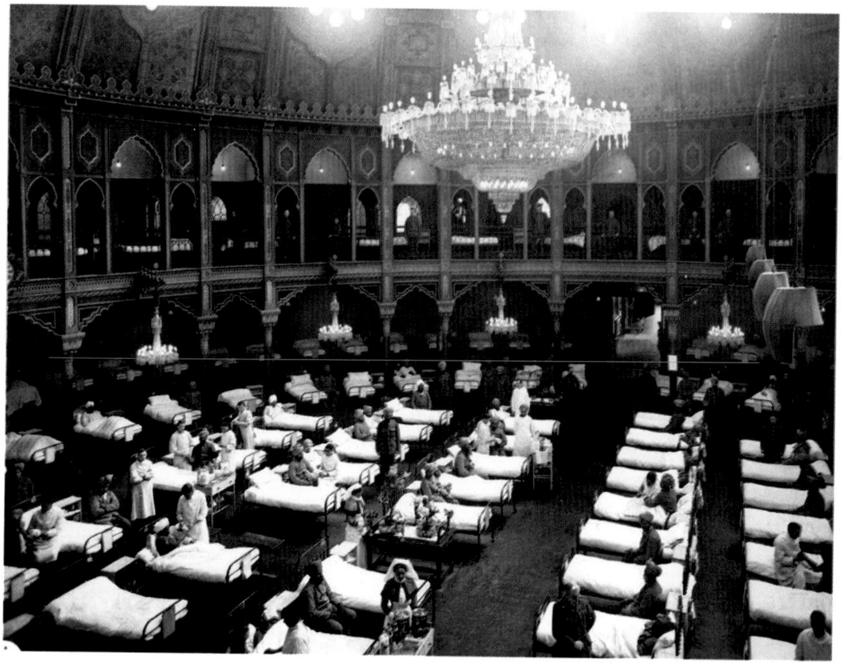

The sumptuous dome auditorium in the Brighton Pavilion was converted into a hospital ward and housed a majority of wounded Indian soldiers. In this picture nurses and doctors can be seen attending to the soldiers under the dome's massive chandeliers.

regiment. At the end of the month Jemadar Moti Singh of the Jodhpur Lancers, and Jemadar Sheonath Singh of the Alwar Lancers, joined the regiment, together with sixty-eight Lancers fron Jodhpur and thirty from Alwar as reinforcements. In September the regiment went into the front line again at Authuile, taking over from the 17th Lancers. The Regimental War Diary records that these were good trenches, situated along the edge of a pine wood and with a good field of fire. Small patrols went out at night in order to learn about the enemy dispositions. The trenches were heavily shelled on 14 September, the kitchen was demolished and the men working there buried; Sowar Sheolal Singh, Sheoju (cook), Tar Singh and Sheo Kamia (workers) were wounded. The position was handed over to the 5th Battalion Gordon Highlanders on 16 September. During this period, Thakur Dalpat Singh and Jemadar Kishen Singh were attached temporarily to the machine gun section of the 18th Lancers in order to learn about the use of this new weapon. News of this development reached India very quickly because on 14 September the colonel received a letter in English from Prithi Singh in Jodhpur, keen to join the regiment. 'I heard that Regent Sahib (Sir Pratab Singh) went to London to get machine guns for our regiment, if so please try and get me there. I heard from Dalpat the other day and he said that he is doing the machine gun course. I will work under him but call me too. I am very anxious to come and join so it is better if you call me.'

The whole of the Indian Cavalry Corps was inspected at Metigny in November, and in December Major R.G.A. Trail of the Queen's Own Corps of Guides joined the Lancers. During the winter of 1915–16 the cavalry worked out a standard organization for holding trenches in the dismounted role and also undertook some mounted training. In January 1916 the GOC of the Indian Cavalry Corps inspected the regiment and expressed his satisfaction with it. However, in March the Corps was broken up and the Jodhpur Lancers became part of the 1st Indian Cavalry Division. There was heavy snow in March but the weather improved in April and the regiment joined in training at the Brigade and divisional level. This training proved to be invaluable when the regiment went to Palestine in 1918. Dafadar Chiman Singh was awarded the Indian Distinguished Service Medal and Sowar Moti Singh the Indian Order of Merit (Second Class). Risaldar Anop Singh and Dafadar Salim Khan were mentioned in despatches. At the opening of the Somme offensive in July 1916 the Division was in reserve behind Gommecourt but, once again, there were few opportunities for mounted action. During the winter of 1916–17 the regiment spent most of its time training, holding part of the line and in the construction of defensive works. For working parties, each brigade provided a battalion named after it, with each regiment contributing a company of 250 men. These working parties brought food, ammunition and other supplies up to the front line and also worked on making new trenches and repairing old ones. Four men were wounded while on working parties in September, and in October and November the regiment went back to brigade and divisional training. There were a number of apparently meaningless changes of billets or bivouac area during this period, of the type familiar to all service men. Nagina Singh of the Jodhpur Cavalry Ambulance wrote home in October 1916: 'We felt the cold here a great deal the first year but now we don't feel it half as much. The Sircar (government) has provided us with so many warm clothes of various kinds that we now prefer the cold weather. When it snows we have great fun and enjoy snowballing each other.'

In spite of their frustration, the officers and men of the Lancers were in no doubt where their duty lay. Kesan Singh, one of the men of the Alwar Lancers serving with the Jodhpur Lancers, wrote home in March 1917: 'You write and press me to return home on leave. My friend, I will return on leave on that day when our Sircar Government is victorious. Till then, I shall never set foot on the homeward road, as I am of the warrior class.' This devotion to authority and the notion of what it means to be a member of the warrior caste is demonstrated in many of the letters written home by Indian soldiers. Balwant Singh of the Jodhpur Lancers wrote in September 1917: 'I am very happy here doing my master's work continually with heart and soul just as my ancestors have always done. We hope that our Government will be victorious and for this we are praying. Besides it is the special duty of a Kshatriya to give his life for his King on the battlefield just as his forefathers did.'

That is not to say that the men forgot their homeland or were unaware of the problems experienced in India at this time. Thakur Dalpat Singh of Deoli, serving with the Jodhpur Lancers, received a letter from home in September 1915: 'This year there is a terrible famine and I would suggest tank-digging and some miscellaneous work as stable roofs, etc., done in the ditch near your museum gate. This will keep your villages intact, otherwise it would take several years to replace them.' Another officer received a letter from a friend in Indore: 'The plague is raging very fiercely and Dala is intending to send all the members of the family off to Ajma. Dala and myself will remain here in a hut or bungalow out of the town if available. All the schools are closed. There has been three inches of rain in Rajasthan in September and it is hoped that the rabi crops will fare well. Famine has been declared and the works have been opened but they say they will have to stop the works since the cultivators have gone to work in the fields. There was to be famine in the Rampura district of Indore state but the rains were very good and so the rabi crops will be good.'

In the spring of 1917 the German Army withdrew to the pre-prepared Hindenburg line in order to shorten their front, and the Indian cavalry took part in a number of skirmishes during the British advance up to this new position. In

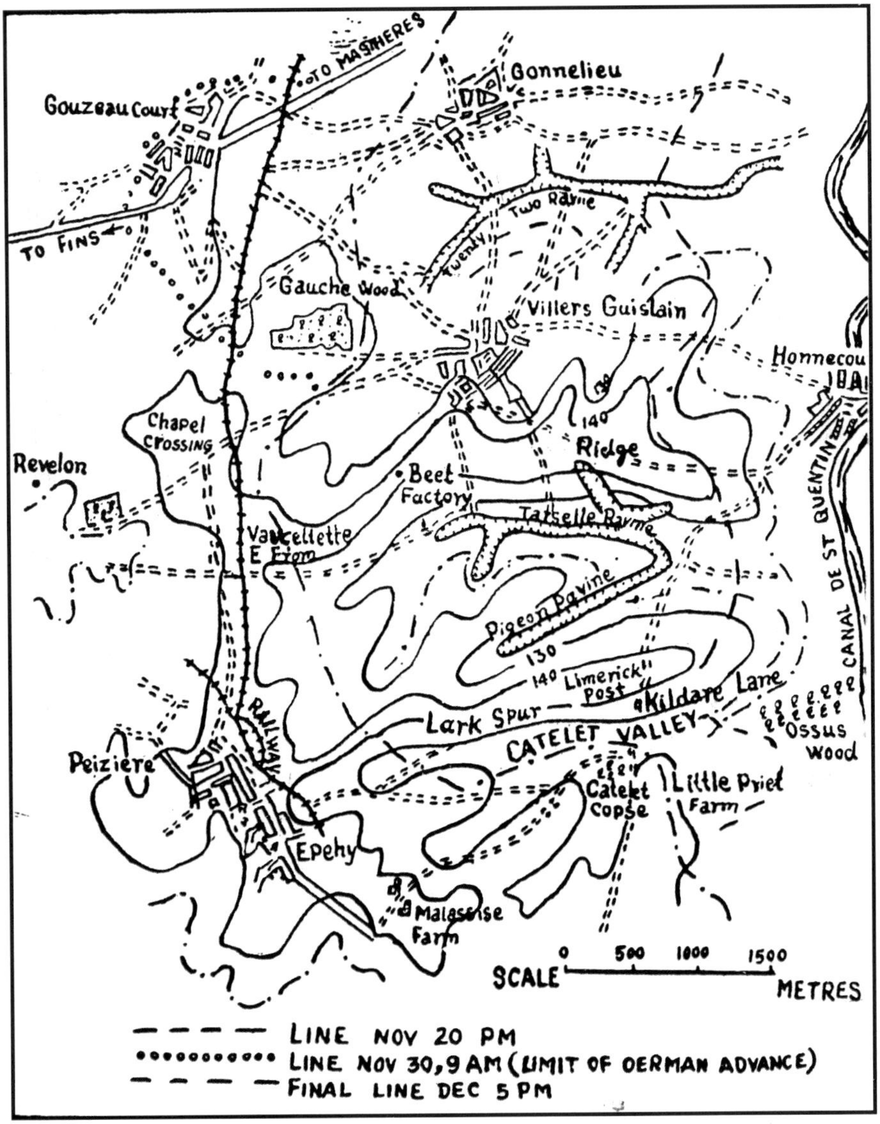

THE BATTLE OF CAMBRAI II WORLD WAR 1
14 APRIL 1915

Map of the Battle of Cambrai.

The village of Witternesse, northern France, where the Lancers were billeted during the winter of 1914–15.

the summer of the same year, the Indian Cavalry Corps was in reserve in case of a breakthrough, but none occurred. In July there was a divisional horse show at which the Jodhpurs won three second prizes and two third prizes. A syce was killed by lightning in August and on 23 September, Lieutenant Daji Raj of the 27th Light Cavalry, who was attached to the regiment, was killed in action. At the end of October the GOC, Lucknow Brigade, inspected four newly promoted Indian officers of the Jodhpur Lancers – Jemadars Bir Singh, Gurdhan Singh, Bhoor Singh and Ragoonath Singh – together with Jemadar Sohan Singh of the Alwar Lancers. He also met Sowar Dhokal Singh, who had received an immediate award of the Indian Order of Merit (Second Class) for 'an act of gallantry in the face of the enemy'. Unfortunately the War Diary says nothing about the nature of his gallantry. In February 1918 Dhokal Singh wrote to a friend in Marwar, modestly playing down his exploit: 'I am very happy here. Through good fortune your humble servant has been able to show brave deeds. Gobind Singh has won the first prize for bravery and after that comes your humble servant. Neither he nor I really did anything but the reputation of our caste for bravery is so great

Vaucelette Farm as it stands today.

that we win rewards.' Gobind Singh (mentioned in the letter) was from Jodhpur, 28th Cavalry, attached to the 2nd Lancers. He was awarded the Victoria Cross for carrying messages under fire during the Battle of Cambrai.

Again in 1917 the advent of winter saw the regiment settle down to trench work and training, interrupted for a short duration by the Cambrai offensive. In November, even while this battle went on, cavalry – including the Jodhpur Lancers – were brought forward along a prepared track. However, their progress was stopped by a canal and they bivouacked on the Hindenburg Line in the vicinity of Vacquerie, which the Germans had relinquished. Major General Sir Pratap once again shared the dangers and discomforts of the men. As luck would have it, the much-longed-for breakthrough failed to materialize and the cavalry were withdrawn, only to be hurriedly brought into action again when the Germans counter-attacked. On 1 December, during heavy fighting, the Lucknow Brigade of the 5th (Indian) Cavalry Division was given orders for a dismounted attack – to be led by nine tanks – on the village of Villers Guislan. The Jodhpur Lancers, together with the 36th (the Jacob's Horse) were to supply the first two

Above and facing page: The Indian War Memorial, Neuve-Chapelle, northern France.

lines of assault, with the 29th Lancers in reserve. The Jodhpurs were to deploy on the left of the road running from Epehy northwards to Villers Guislan while the Jacob's Horse deployed on the right of the road! (See map). The attack was to take place at 6.30 a.m. but the tanks failed to appear. The plan was therefore changed so that the 36th alone would advance on Villers Guislan from Vaucelette Farm, with the other two regiments in reserve. The advance was met by heavy enemy fire and came to a stop about 100 metres beyond the farm. There was no British artillery support and machine guns could not be brought to bear on the German positions. At 10.30 a.m. the Jodhpurs were ordered forward to support the 36th, who were working along the railway line running to the north of the farm. At this point Major Trail was severely wounded while liaising with the 36th. At 2.30 p.m. the Lancers and the 36th were ordered to concentrate at the farm, with a view to attacking the sugar beet factory south of Villers Guislan – with the Jodhpurs on the left, joining up with a Canadian machine gun unit to their right if possible. All the time the regiment was under heavy machine gun

1914 FRANCE & FLANDERS 1918
LA BASSEE 1914
MESSINES 1914
ARMENTIERES 1914
YPRES 1914-15
GHELUVELT
FESTUBERT 1914-15
GIVENCHY 1914
NEUVE CHAPELLE
ST JULIEN
AUBERS
LOOS
SOMME 1916
BAZENTIN
DELVILLE WOOD
FLERS-COURCELETTE
MORVAL
CAMBRAI 1917

fire, together with high-explosive and shrapnel gun fire. The attack could not progress further than about 700 metres east of the farm and when darkness fell the Brigade dug in there and was relieved during the night.

The ground is little changed today and the visitor can easily understand the difficulties facing the attacking troops. The railway line is still in place; there are additional modern farm buildings at Vaucelette Farm and the sugar beet factory is a ruin, but one can easily understand the latter's importance as a forward position for the Germans. There is a slight ridge between the farm and the village; the enemy machine gunners would have had a clear field of fire as the Indians moved forward towards them. Advancing over open ground without the tanks and without proper artillery support meant that the attack was doomed from the start. In the context of the war in general, this was just a little skirmish, hardly worth a sentence in the Divisional Report, but it cost the regiment the lives of Sowars Bagh Khan, Bhairon Singh, Hamid Khan, Sohan Singh, Major Trail and an unnamed sowar – possibly Ladu Khan, who died on 4 December. An unnamed Indian officer and eighteen sowars were wounded. Major R.G.A. Trail (Guides Cavalry), who had been recently appointed a special service officer with the regiment, died later of his wounds and is buried in the nearby military cemetery at Tincourt. The regiment was withdrawn into reserve at 8.30 p.m. Bir Singh wrote home on 20 December: 'We have 21 wounded in our regiment, five of them mortally.' Cambrai was to be the last battle for the regiment in France, though they did not leave the country until April 1918. The fighting cost the Lancers four killed, twenty-three wounded and one man missing.

Overall the experience of the regiment, and indeed of all of the cavalry – both Indian and British – in France had been frustrating. The trench warfare, the

Facing page and above: Graves of Jodhpur Lancers in northern France.

often appalling condition of the ground, which was frequently waterlogged and churned up by constant shelling, together with thick barbed wire entanglements, made a cavalry charge virtually impossible. When combined with heavy machine gun and shell fire, it became suicidal. On only a handful of occasions on the Western Front were cavalry employed in the mounted role and never in large numbers. Much of their time was spent in billets, training or undertaking tasks such as trench-digging, and the most frequent comment for these three years in the Regimental War Diary is 'Nothing of importance to report'. Sir Pratap wrote: 'Whenever I met the Generals I used to ask them when the cavalry charge will take place and they always said it would come about soon but it never came about as I wished.' However, the regiment had learned much while in France and that was to stand them in good stead when they left for the Middle East, where they were to earn undying fame.

Chapter 4

THEIR FINEST HOUR: PALESTINE 1918

'*The* [Indian cavalry] *regiments from France had nothing whatsoever to learn from the mounted troops they came alongside in Palestine and could show the way to most.*'

COLONEL E.B. MAUNSELL
The Scinde Horse

Turkey, spurred on by offers of cash and military support from Germany, declared war on Great Britain and France in October 1914. The Turks were hoping to end their diplomatic isolation with German aid, and to regain the territories they had lost in the Balkans. The Germans, on the other hand, had dreams of extending their sphere of influence through the states of the Balkans and Turkey into Persia. The entry of Turkey into the war posed a threat to the Suez Canal, a vital trade route connecting Great Britain with India and beyond. British and Indian troops were sent immediately to strengthen the garrison defending the Canal. However, this

Facing page: Sir Pratap, at the age of sixty-nine (in 1914) stayed with the Jodhpur Lancers throughout the war, leading from the front.

wasn't the only issue. The Sultan of Turkey was Khalif of Islam, and Muslim soldiers from the Indian Army might well have had reservations about fighting Turkish soldiers, who were their co-religionists. Indeed there were a number of desertions, especially amongst Pathans, who came from across the border with Afghanistan. Nevertheless, many Muslim soldiers continued to fight bravely in France and East Africa. Turkish troops, backed by German officers, were a force to reckon with, going by their exploits at Gallipoli and in Mesopotamia.

In November 1914 a large Turkish force moved down through Palestine, crossed the Sinai Desert and attacked the defended strong points along the Canal. By February they had been forced to retreat. The Allied troops moved forward into Sinai to put up a stronger defence but were unable to make much headway against the Turkish forces. In July 1917 General Allenby arrived in Palestine and adopted more aggressive tactics, capturing Jerusalem by Christmas. Consequently in January 1918, the Turkish army in Palestine – some 36,000 strong – held two sectors extending from the Mediterranean to the Dead Sea and separated by the River Jordan. In 1918 the Indian cavalry regiments were transferred to Egypt from France. They were brigaded with British yeomanry regiments and joined the Desert Mounted Corps, consisting of the 4th and 5th Cavalry Divisions, together with the Australian Mounted Division. The Jodhpur Lancers landed in Egypt on 28 March 1918. They joined the Mysore and the Hyderabad Lancers – replacing the Patiala Lancers, who had gone to Mesopotamia – in the 15th (Imperial Service) Cavalry Brigade of the 5th Division. The brigade included an artillery battery from the British Honourable Artillery Company. By May 1918 two brigades from the 4th and 5th Divisions, now re-armed with lances, were amid the unpleasant summer conditions of the Jordan Valley, where they were involved in a number of successful patrol actions. Later they were joined by three other brigades. There was then some reorganization of the cavalry before the final offensive, which was planned for September and whose aim was to totally destroy the Turkish forces in Palestine, Syria and Lebanon. Following an infantry attack, the cavalry were to advance along the Palestine coast, break through the Turkish defences and then turn north-eastwards over the Carmel Range and down into the plain of Megiddo. An elaborate deception plan effectively confused the Turks as to the direction of the main thrust. The cavalry moved forward on the night of 18 September. The surprise was total and the Hodson's Horse,

HH Maharaja Sumer Singh in the Jodhpur Lancers uniform.
It was in his name that the regiment fought at Haifa.

acting as the advance guard, was through the main enemy defences by 6.00 a.m. the next morning. By the evening of 20 September, the 4th Cavalry Division was astride the main communication line between the Turkish 7th and 6th Armies and Damascus. Phase One of the operation had been completed in 36 hours and the Division had advanced 110 kilometres. Acre was captured on 23 September

The Lancers moving through Haifa.

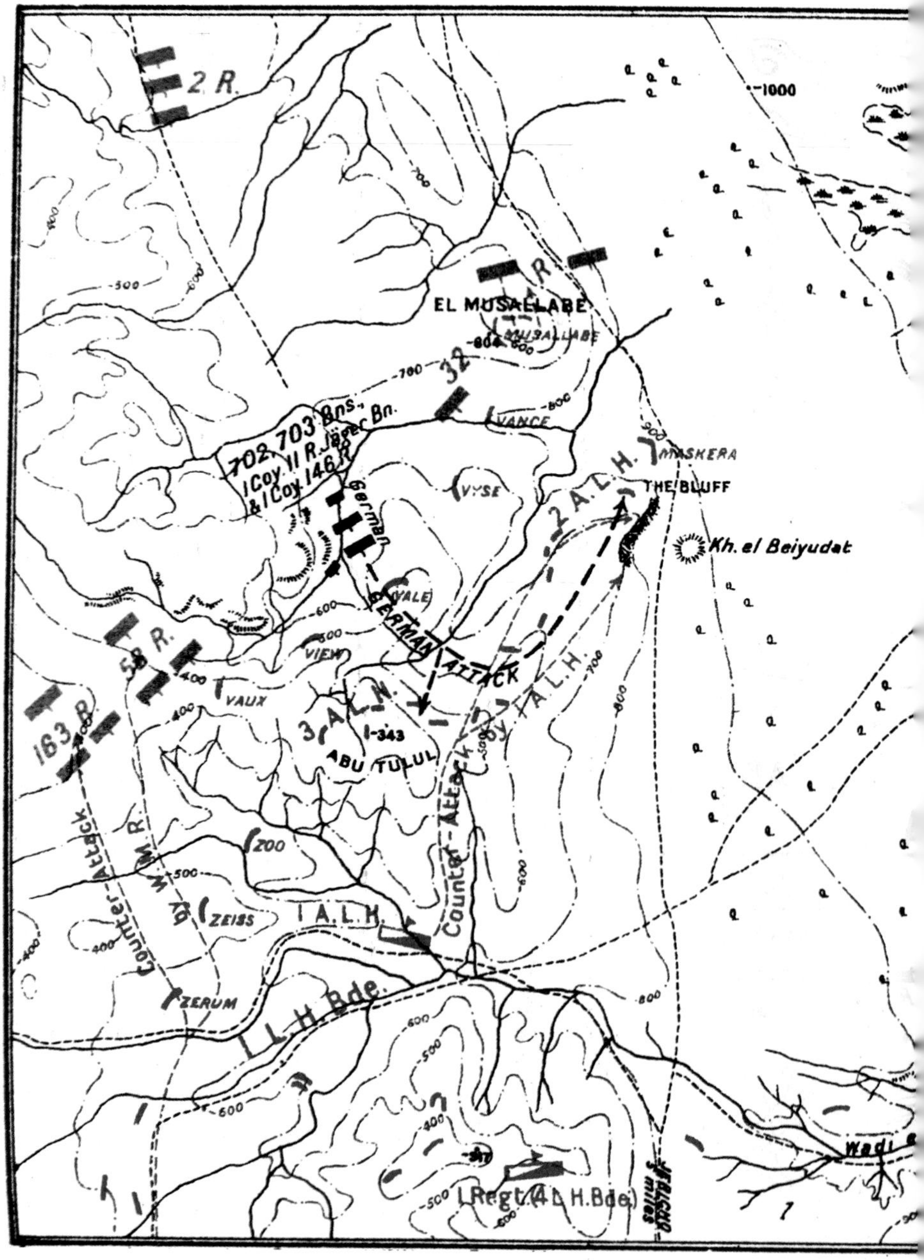
2 R.
EL MUSALLABE
MUSALLABE
32
VANCE
702, 703 Bns.,
Jäger Bn.
1 Coy. 11 R.
& 1 Coy. 146 R.
Germans
MASKERA
THE BLUFF
2 A.L.H.
Kh. el Beiyudat
VYSE
VALE
GERMAN ATTACK
VIEW
58 R.
163 R.
VAUX
3 A.L.H.
ABU TULUL
Counter-Attack by 1 A.L.H.
Counter-Attack by W.M.R.
ZOO
ZEISS
1 A.L.H.
ZERUM
L.H. Bde.
1 Regt. (4 L.H. Bde.)
Wadi

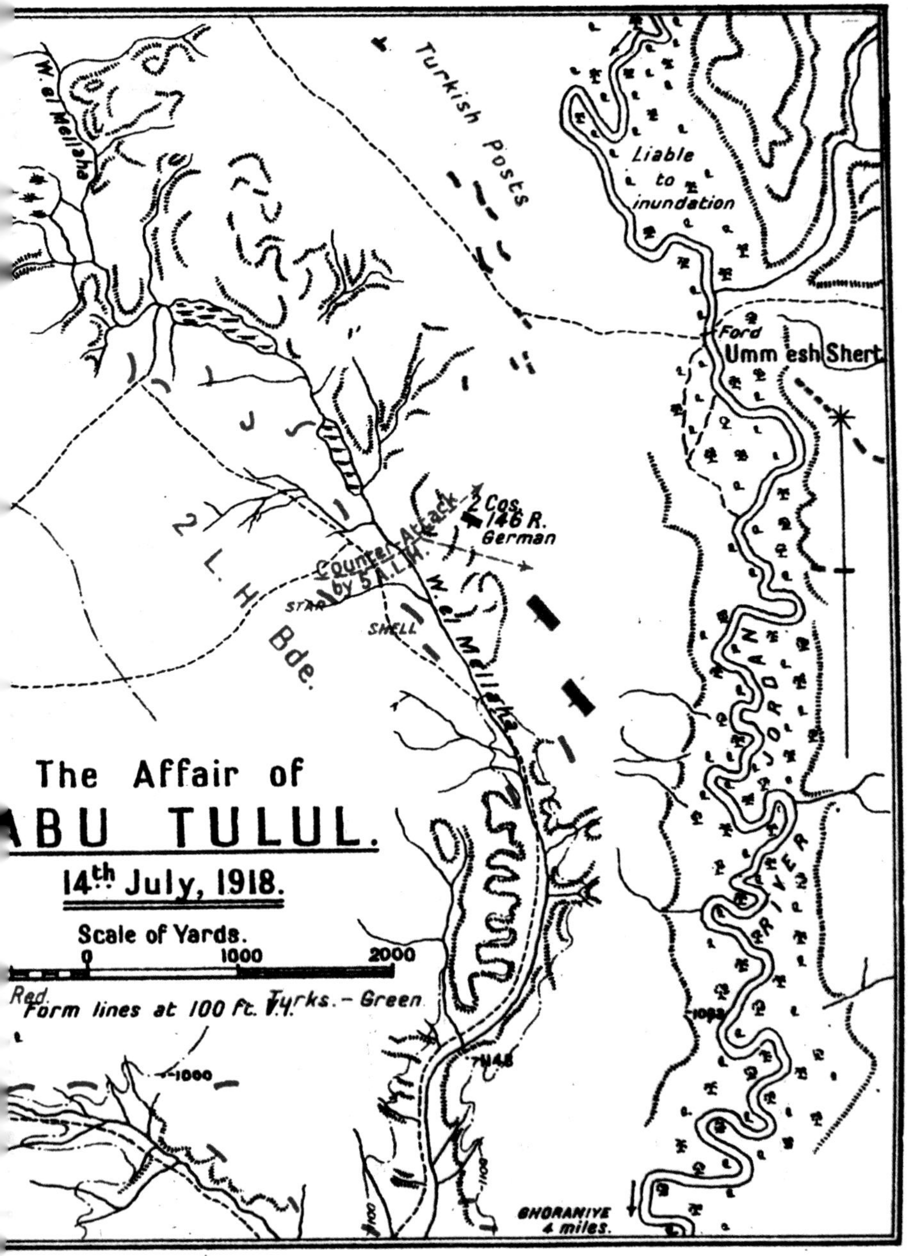

Map of the battle that took place at Abu Tulul. Bored with the trenches of France and itching for some real cavalry fighting, the Lancers showed their mettle in their very first action at Abu Tulul on 14 July.

and Haifa on the same day by the Jodhpur Lancers. On 26 September the Desert Mounted Corps began their advance upon Damascus, which was captured on 1 October. In just over a month, the Corps, including thirteen Indian regiments out of a total of twenty-four, had destroyed three Turkish armies and taken 46,000 prisoners.

The Jodhpur Lancers arrived in Egypt under the command of Major Thakur Pratab Singh; Colonel Maharaj Sher Singh having returned to India to take command of the Depot – the regimental base in India – which had grown considerably in size. While in Egypt, and before the regiment went into action again, the opportunity to play some polo could not be missed. In order to clear the stones from a level piece of ground, the Lancers requisitioned 400 labourers' baskets – normally used for entrenching work – from Royal Engineer stores. The sowars, each with a basket, lined up at one end of the polo ground. They moved slowly across the ground, picking up every stone, and some excellent polo followed. After this pleasant and well-deserved break, the regiment was moved by rail through Sinai to the Jordan Valley, where it joined the Brigade on 11 May, relieving a New Zealand regiment, the Wellington Mounted Rifles. On the 16th a Lancer patrol captured four prisoners right in front of the Turkish trenches and a day later the Brigade marched to a bivouac area, one mile north of Jericho. Mounted training commenced and reconnaissance patrols were undertaken by the British and Indian officers of all points where the Brigade might be called upon to counter-attack. The machine gun subsection of the Jodhpurs joined those from the Mysore and Hyderabad regiments to form a machine gun squadron for the Brigade. Conditions in the Jordan Valley were very bad. The atmosphere was oppressive, with temperatures up to 55 degrees centigrade; the dust worried both horses and men; and there were many flies and mosquitoes close to the river.

In June the Jodhpur Lancers were moved to a more healthy climate but in July returned to the Valley to occupy part of the bridgehead over the Jordan, which secured the British right flank. Here there were two swing bridges across the Jordan: the southern one, at Henu, close to the junction between the river, and the Wadi El Rameh, which itself was passable at Sangster's Ford. The Jodhpurs were responsible for the southern bridgehead while the northern bridge at El Hajla was covered by the Mysore Lancers. At last, after the frustration of the previous three years, the regiment was being given their first real opportunity

Major Thakur Dalpat Singh during his time at Eastbourne College.

to show just what they could do. At 3.30 a.m. on the morning of 14 July, the regiment's standing patrol of nine men on the eastern bank of the river was attacked by the advance guard of the 2nd Turkish Caucasian Cavalry Brigade. The patrol opened fire on the enemy, wounding an officer and killing his horse. 'A' squadron (about eighty men) crossed the Wadi El Rameh at Sangster's Ford in support of the patrol but themselves came under heavy fire. Fortunately there were no casualties and the men got themselves under cover. The Jodhpurs attempted to push southwards while the Turks moved northwards with a view to getting behind 'A' squadron and cutting them off. As the enemy came out of the hills to the east at 1,200 yards range they were brought under heavy fire by the Lancers using both rifles and Hotchkiss machine guns. A troop under Jemadar Chotu Singh was ordered to take up a firing position, which they did, killing many Turks through the day. The machine-gunner Dafadar Amer Singh earned himself the Indian Order of Merit (Second Class).

By 8.00 a.m. it was realized that 'A' Squadron had at least 300 of the enemy in front of them from the 9th and 11th Turkish Cavalry Regiments, with the 7th Cavalry Regiment in reserve. Pushing out patrols, the Lancers were able to locate the whole of the enemy's position over a frontage of two miles and also to establish the number of machine guns facing them. Meanwhile, a squadron of the Mysore Lancers, accompanied by two Australian Lewis guns, was trying to push forward through the northern bridgehead at Hajla. Two squadrons of the Jodhpur Lancers were ordered to assemble, cross the Jordan at Henu and to roll up the enemy position from south to north. At 12.10 p.m. the advance began with one troop under Jemadar Khang Singh in the lead. The squadrons (some 125 men) moved steadily south-eastwards, taking advantage of a dry valley as cover. Once in position, they turned north and galloped straight over the first objective. Seeing the advance of the unstoppable Jo Hokums, three troops of Turkish cavalry on the extreme right flank immediately made off to the east.

The leading troop thundered ahead towards their second objective, killing all the enemy there. Meanwhile the rest of the Lancers made for the next ridge further east, which was covered with Turkish troops. It was here that the stiffest fighting took place, with many individual acts of bravery. Major Dalpat Singh, leading the charge and accompanied only by his trumpet major, went full-tilt for an enemy machine gun, killing the gunners and capturing the gun. He later captured the commandant of the 11th Turkish Regiment. He was awarded the Military Cross for his leadership and courage on that day – one of the first Indian officers to be thus honoured. The citation for his award reads: 'For conspicuous gallantry and devotion to duty. This officer, accompanied only by his trumpeter, charged an entrenched machine gun, killing and scattering the crew and capturing the gun. At the same time he captured the commandant of a regiment and another officer.'

Dalpat Singh, who had spent four years at Eastbourne College in England (sponsored by Sir Pratap), was the eldest son of Thakur Hari (Hurjee) Singh of

Sir Pratap's second son, 2nd Lieutenant Kanwar Sagat Singh, MC, was awarded one of the two Military Crosses in the Palestine campaign.

Deoli. Hari Singh commanded the Jodhpur Lancers and served in the Tirah, Black Mountain and China campaigns. He was a fine polo player – a member of the team which won the Indian championship in 1893 – and a close friend of Sir Pratap. While at school, Dalpat Singh had excelled in cricket, and was awarded his First Eleven Colours in three successive years. He was a Lance-Corporal in the College Officer Training Corps. The 1911 issue of the School Magazine – also his last year at school, during which he scored a century playing against South Lynn – carried the comment: 'Dalpat Singh has played some fine innings during the term and got runs with great consistency. His cutting and leg glides were excellent. He was also first rate slip and a bowler who often had a good day.'

On his return to India Dalpat Singh became an equally good polo player and a favourite of Sir Pratap's. He joined the regiment as a squadron commander in October 1914.

Risaldar Shaitan Singh, out in front of his troop at the second ridge, single-handedly attacked a large group of about fifty enemies. Once he got into the enemy position, his men followed him, killing a great number and capturing fourteen of them. Shaitan Singh had shot two men with his revolver when one of the prisoners tried to shoot him, the bullet going through his horse's jaw. Singh's revolver was empty but he was able to knock the Turk to the ground with his weighted stick. Initially the sowars were intent on taking prisoners, but when a dafadar was shot in the back by a prisoner who picked up a rifle, no quarter was given. After this second ridge was cleared, the regiment was ordered to advance onto the final objective, where more of the enemy were killed or captured, with the machine gun section killing many Turks. The citation for Risaldar Shaitan Singh's Indian Order of merit reads as follows: 'For conspicous gallantry and initiative on 14th July 1918 when serving with the Egyptian Expeditionary Force in delivering an immediate mounted attack on the enemy. Accompanied by three men, he charged a formed body of about thirty dismounted enemy, killed and wounded fourteen and captured the officer in command.'

After the second objective had been taken, Jemadars Assu Singh and Khang Singh, along with the former's troop, crossed the rear of the main advance and swung further out to the east. Seeing a force of the enemy trying to escape, they charged them without hesitation and tried to cut them off. Unfortunately for the Lancers, the enemy – two squadrons of Turks together with some Germans –

turned around and the whole of Assu Singh's troop was destroyed, fighting to the last. Only two wounded men survived. Both the jemadars were killed and both were awarded the Indian Order of Merit (Second Class) posthumously.

Anticipating a counter-attack from the large number of Turks still in the field, the regiment fell back towards the river. 'A' Squadron sent out patrols to keep the enemy under observation and also to retrieve the dead and wounded Lancers. Later the regiment was relieved by the Hyderabad Lancers. One hundred from the enemy side had been killed or wounded and seventy were taken prisoner, this for the loss of two Indian officers killed and one wounded, thirteen sowars killed, seven wounded and five missing. In addition to Major Dalpat Singh's immediate award of a Military Cross, six Indian Orders of Merit (Second Class) and seven Indian Distinguished Service Medals were distributed amongst the Lancers (see Appendix 5). General Allenby, who visited the Brigade on 27 August 1918, wrote: 'The day's operations would live on as one of the great feats of the war.' The Brigade History comments: 'The success gained was mainly due to the spirited action, dash and able leadership displayed in the mounted attack by five troops of the Jodhpur Lancers.'

At a ceremonial parade of the regiment at their camp in the Jordon Valley on 25 August, Sir Pratap conveyed the congratulations of the maharaja and presented medals to those who had been decorated. However, in spite of the regiment's great success, he was very disappointed that his son, Sagat Singh, the Adjutant of the Lancers, had stayed by the telephone at regimental headquarters and had not taken part in the charge. He refused to speak to Sagat Singh and when Major Gill, one of the British officers serving with the regiment, explained that Sagat Singh had been acting on his orders, he refused to speak to him as well. Sir Pratap was also displeased that not all of the Lancers had taken part in the charge as some provided a firing line in support of their comrades. He told General Harbord, commanding the Brigade, 'Next time you make the Mysore and Hyderabad Lancers do fire action and the whole of the Jodhpur Lancers charge!'

Chapter 5

THE CAPTURE OF HAIFA

'An event unprecedented in war!'

Paintings of the eighteenth- and nineteenth-century battles often depict dashing cavalry charges, for instance of the charge of the Scots Greys at Waterloo by Lady Butler. The sad fact, however, is that the majority of these charges – that of the Scots Greys included – failed to achieve their objective. The French cavalry at Waterloo were unable to penetrate a single British infantry square despite their repeated attempts. The success of the Hanoverian Dragoons of the King's German Legion at Garci Hernandez in Spain, in breaking a French infantry square, was possible only because a wounded horse fell into the square, creating an opening for the horsemen. Then, as the more accurate rifle replaced the musket and the machine gun found its way into the battlefield, it became virtually impossible for cavalry to break a stand by disciplined infantry in a good defensive position.

The Turkish infantry and artillery at Haifa had the advantage of defending a strong position within buildings which could easily be fortified, and this is what makes the success of the Jodhpur Lancers here all the more remarkable. Success

Facing page: Breech of a cannon captured by the Jodhpur Lancers at Haifa – today lies at Sardar Samand Palace, near Jodhpur.

in such a scenario would depend greatly upon speed and determination, attributes which the Lancers seemed to be amply endowed with. In 1916, a Rajput trooper serving in France had received a letter that appeared to have been written by a member of his family – possibly his father – which included the following passage: 'You are a Rajput whose duty it is to die on the battlefield if necessary and thus secure paradise. For a Rajput to die on horseback is a matter for pride.' Hence, it was in this spirit that the Jo Hokums charged at Haifa.

During the weeks that followed the Lancers' action at El Henu, a new and larger bridgehead, containing both the old Hajla and Henu bridgeheads, was constructed and wired in, while active patrolling into the hills to the east continued. The regiment underwent a period of intensive regimental and brigade training until mid-September and the Desert Corps was reorganized for the final offensive. On the evening of 17 September, the regiment bivouacked in an orange grove, secure from observation by the enemy from the air. An intensive artillery bombardment opened on the Turkish positions at 4.30 a.m. on 19 September. The Turks were taken by surprise and by 8.30 a.m. their trenches were captured and the British and Indian infantry began their wheel to the right, away from the sea. Following the infantry breakthrough, the cavalry were to advance along the coast, at times actually on the beach. The 5th Cavalry Division was ordered to capture Haifa and Acre, ports which were urgently needed in order to shorten the army's over-stretched supply lines. The Royal Navy had command of the Mediterranean and military stores could be brought directly into these two ports instead of having to be carried overland across the Sinai from Suez. They started their advance at 3.00 a.m. on 23 September, with the 13th Brigade advancing along the Nazareth-Acre road while the other two brigades of the Division moved towards Haifa with the 15th (IS) Brigade in the lead. The Hyderabad Lancers were ordered to escort a very large group of enemy prisoners to the rear and the Brigade (minus the Hyderabad Lancers) was accompanied by 'B' Battery of the Honourable Artillery Company (HAC).

As the Imperial Service Brigade moved forward, no enemy were sighted until the advanced guard of the Mysore Lancers reached the village of Beled Esh Sheikh at about 10.00 a.m., where they were shelled by enemy guns on Mount Carmel and fired upon by machine guns and snipers to the west of the village. A British aeroplane dropped a message saying that Haifa was strongly held. The

Jodhpur Lancers were ordered to make a mounted attack to capture the town while the one squadron of the Mysore Lancers worked along the ridge of Mount Carmel behind the town. Because of the difficult ascent, only fifteen men from the Mysore Lancers made their final charge along the ridge but they captured three guns, two machine guns and 78 prisoners. The Jodhpurs were to attack at 2.00 p.m., keeping north of the railway line, with fire support from the artillery and two squadrons of the Mysore Lancers on the plain. The Sherwood Rangers (a British Yeomanry regiment) joined the Brigade at 11.45 a.m. and one of their squadrons was ordered forward to support the Mysore Lancers on the mountain.

The town of Haifa faces north across a bay, and behind the town Mount Carmel rises steeply to a height of about 200 feet. Access to the town is along a narrow gap between the ridge and the River Kishon, which feeds into the sea. Through this defile runs a road and a railway going north to Acre with a spur into Haifa.

The ground around the River Kishon was very soft and its banks very steep, making it impassable for mounted men. According to official history: 'The position was naturally formidable with a precipitous hill and an impassable river on either side of a defile. It was held by a well-armed force of about one thousand strong which had not yet been engaged.' To order a cavalry regiment to attack a defended town was asking a great deal. To send them to attack the town through a defile would form a natural killing ground for the enemy machine-gunners and invite them to charge to almost certain death. There were very few other examples, if any, throughout history, of cavalry capturing a defended town. Only forty years before this, the fate of the French cuirassiers shot down by Prussian infantry in Morsbron had shown just what could happen to a cavalry caught in a built-up area.

The Jo Hokums, however, were undaunted. At noon the four squadrons of the Jodhpurs moved off in line of troop columns, halting briefly at Yajur, and patrols – that were fired upon by the Turks – were sent out to check whether it was possible to cross the river. The regiment then advanced at the appointed time, shells bursting around them, and as they continued steadily forward, machine guns opened up on them from the lower slopes of Mount Carmel as well as from a position to the north of the railway. On crossing the railway line running northwards to Acre, the regiment changed formation into columns of troops with three paces between the files. On reaching the river, with its very steep banks, two scouts were swallowed up by quicksand. One squadron moved northwards in a futile attempt to find a crossing, while the rest of the regiment, realizing that it was impossible to cross the river at this point, moved forward, increasing their pace and slightly left shouldering as they went. It was here that Major Dalpat Singh was fatally wounded.

It became clear that the only way to continue the advance was to first open up the defile by destroying the machine guns on Mount Carmel and then to clear the position to the north of the railway line leading into the town. 'B' Squadron, made up of Jodha Rathores, was in the lead at this point and was ordered to attack the position on the hill. This was the critical moment, as concentrated enemy fire was bringing down a number of the Lancers' horses. The squadron nonetheless charged fearlessly, spearing all the machine gunners, scattering the riflemen and capturing two machine guns and two camel guns. This highly successful charge opened up the defile and 'D' Squadron, which was following 'B' Squadron, galloped straight down the road towards the town before swinging half-right to take the position to the north of the railway line. They too were successful, capturing four howitzers and four machine guns. However, their squadron commander, Anop Singh, had two horses shot from under him. Meanwhile the remaining two squadrons rode undeterred, at full speed, straight through the town. The fight was practically over once the defile was forced, though there were occasional shots from the houses and a few Turks were ridden down. Once beyond the town, the regiment reformed. In all, two German officers, twenty-three Turkish officers and 664 other ranks were captured. Two six-inch naval guns, ten field guns and ten machine guns were also taken. This tremendous success was achieved at the cost of Major Dalpat Singh's life and that of two sowars; five officers and twenty-nine other men were wounded; and sixty horses were killed and eighty-three wounded. The number of horses killed and wounded gives some idea of the intensity of fire faced by the men in their charge.

There is an interesting footnote to the charge. Men of the 15th Field Troop of the Royal Engineers had been busy removing demolition charges from railway bridges during the Brigade's advance. They chanced to be alongside the Jodhpur Lancers as the latter were ordered to charge. The Lancers' commanding officer invited Sergeant Hearne and his sappers to arm themselves with swords and lances from the wounded men. None of the engineers had ever handled these weapons but they took their position on the right of the line and it is reported

Major Thakur Dalpat Singh, the Hero of Haifa, first served as scout officer and adjutant with the regiment in France before he was appointed squadron commander.

that at least one Turk was killed by them. This appears to be the only occasion in their long and distinguished history that the Royal Engineers took part in a cavalry charge.

By any standard, the capture of Haifa on 23 September 1918 by the Jodhpur Lancers was a magnificent feat of arms and unique in military history. The French General Lasalle, with his Hussars, had captured the Prussian town of Stettin in 1806 but that was through sheer bluff. The official history of the campaign comments: 'No more remarkable cavalry action of its scale was fought in the whole course of the campaign.' The brigade major, Major Charles Hervey,

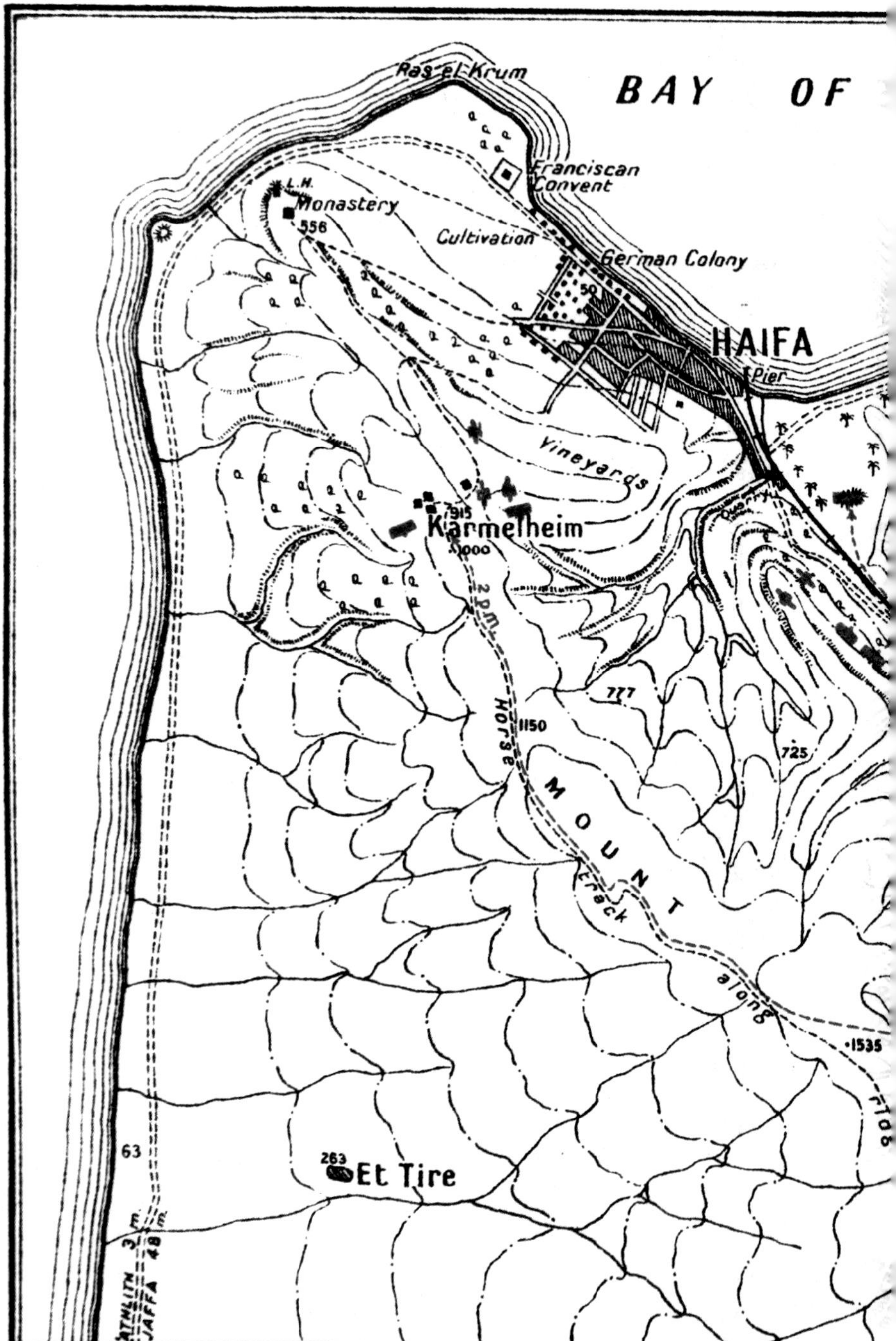

BAY OF
Ras el Krum
Franciscan Convent
L.H.
Monastery
556
Cultivation
German Colony
HAIFA
Pier
Vineyards
Quarry
915
Karmelheim
Horse
Track
along
MOUNT
777
1150
725
1535
63
263
Et Tire
ATHLITH 3m
JAFFA 48m

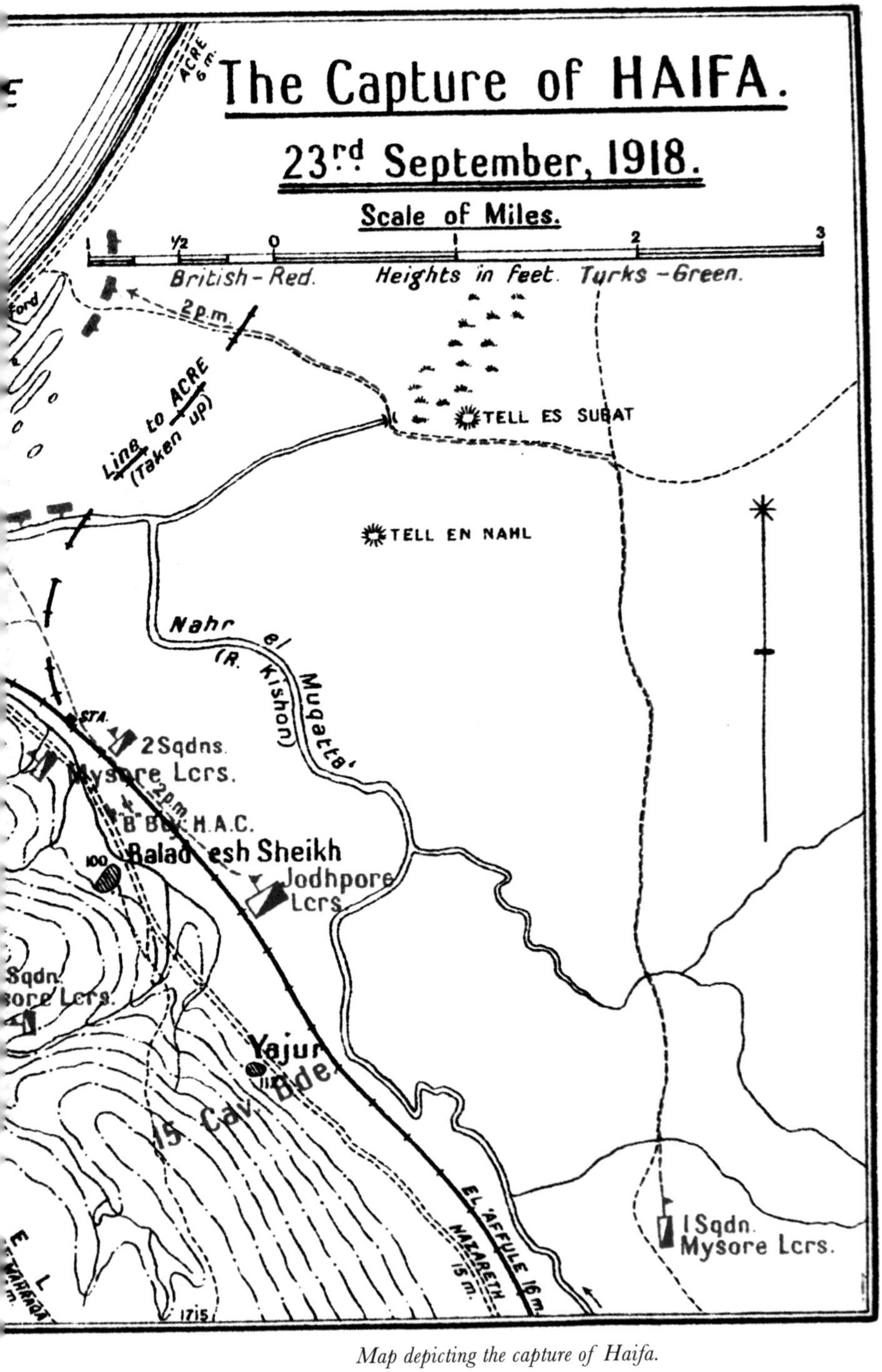

Map depicting the capture of Haifa.

wrote to his parents in England: 'I suppose it is the best example of how cavalry should be used, and of their value, that there has ever been in history. It was the speed at which we came round that did it. It will make people see what Indian cavalry can do. We galloped at a place which anyone who saw the ground would have thought it impregnable. However, a stout hearted body of men on galloping horses take a lot of stopping and within half an hour from the word go, Haifa was ours.'

The Lancers' outstanding achievement was certainly recognized by senior British officers. Major General MacAndrew, commanding the 5th Cavalry Division, wrote to Sir Pratap on 24 September: 'I am very sorry to tell you that Major Dalpat Singh died of wounds last night. He led the regiment with great dash and was killed by machine gun fire while galloping across the river into Haifa. The Jodhpur Lancers as usual did splendidly. Their charge across the river with 8 machine guns and six guns firing on them was a great sight. I am so sorry that you had fever and were not with us. I hope to see you back soon. The enemy fought better than any we have met yet. Your regiment had 1 officer (Dalpat) killed and two wounded, 3 men killed and 30 wounded.' General Allenby telegraphed on the same day: 'Congratulate you on the brilliant exploit of your regiment the Jodhpur Lancers who on the 23rd September took the town of Haifa at a gallop, killing many Turks with the lance in the streets of the town and capturing seven hundred prisoners. Their gallant Colonel Dalpat Singh fell gloriously at the head of his regiment. He was buried with full military honours this afternoon.'

When Dalpat Singh first went to England as a small boy, to be educated, he stayed with the Reverend and Mrs Tudor in Willingdon near Eastbourne. Major Hervey (the brigade major) wrote to Mrs Tudor on 3 October 1918: 'You will doubtless have heard by now that Dalpat Singh died in the early morning of 24 September from wounds he received on 23 September when gallantly leading his regiment in a mounted attack on Haifa.... All went well until they got near the town when they were blocked by an impassable river. Colonel Holden, who was leading, shouted to Dalpat to wheel the regiment to the left. At that moment, Dalpat was hit in the spine by a machine gun bullet and fell. The machine gunner did not live long after firing that shot; the leading squadron galloped straight at him and killed him in a second. The whole regiment was mad with rage and took a lot of cooling down. They carried him into Haifa but he died next morning on

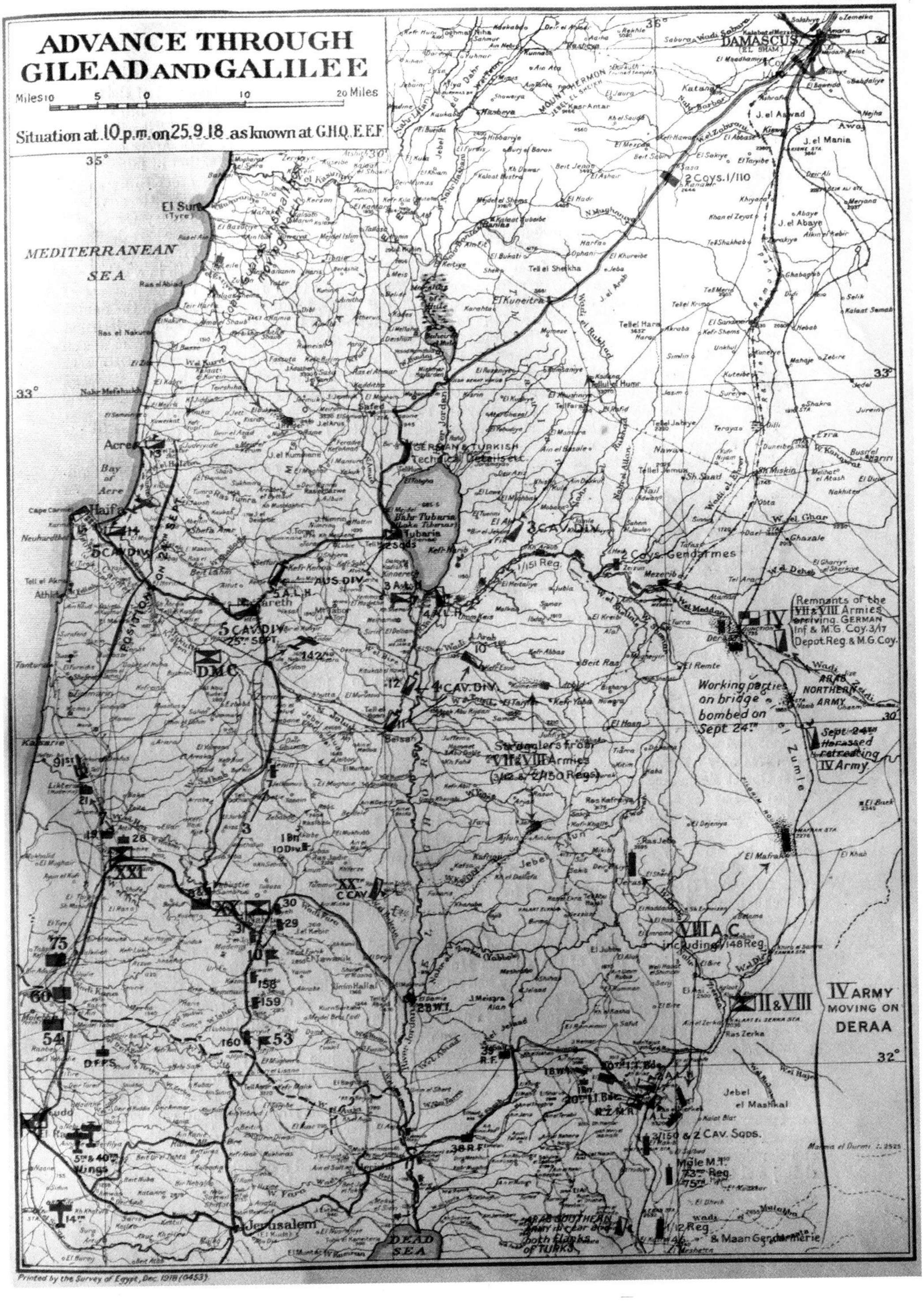

Printed by the Survey of Egypt, Dec. 1918 (0453).

War memorial at Eastbourne College, which includes Dalpat Singh's name.

M. H. BYTHWAY
C. P. G. CAMERON
R. S. CARLTON
C. M. CAZALET
R. E. CHANDLER
A. D. CLARK
M. T. CLARKE
A. D. COLLINS
D. T. COUSINS
A. N. COXE
M. E. COXHEAD
L. F. COXSON
T. DALPAT SINGH
T. G. DE DENNE
C. H. M. DENNYS
E. M. DENNYS
H. C. DE PINNA
O. S. DITZEN
N. DODD
K. M. DOUGLAS
R. G. DYER

the operating table. We buried him that afternoon, in an olive grove, at the south end of the city, looking out to sea. His death is a loss not only to Sir Pratab who adored him, and to all the Jodhpurs, but to India.'

Dalpat Singh is buried in the Commonwealth War Graves Commission Cemetery in Haifa. His name is recorded on the Memorial Tablets in an impressive archway under the tower of the building built in the 1920s as a memorial to the Old Boys of Eastbourne College, who fell in the Great War.

It is inexplicable why the Lancers have not received greater recognition for this action, especially when viewed against the awards they were given after the fight at the Henu bridgehead. They were not awarded a battle honour for Haifa; only the more general honour 'Megiddo'. There may be several reasons for this. By a dreadful irony, Sir Pratap was not present at the charge, having gone down with fever on 20 September, and returning to India shortly afterwards. Perhaps it was felt that the regiment had already been sufficiently rewarded for the earlier engagement. Also, as the war was to end in a few more weeks, the genuine claims of the regiment were perhaps overlooked or forgotten. Certainly no evidence has emerged of any request for a battle honour or for decorations to be awarded to those who took part. Moreover, British interest had always been focused, necessarily, on the defeat of the Germans on the Western Front. Whatever the explanation, the Jodhpur Lancers have every reason to be proud of their unrivalled triumph at Haifa. Their descendants, the 61st Cavalry, quite rightly still celebrate Haifa Day on 23 September as one of the most important days in the regimental calendar. After a ceremonial parade in full dress and a banquet, there are sports and games – including, of course, polo.

Sir Pratap never forgave himself for not being with the regiment at their finest hour. He also seemed to have some foreknowledge of Dalpat's death. His son, Rao Raja Hanut Singh, later recounted a story of how he had found Sir Pratap in tears on the morning of 24 September, saying, 'Dalpat's great day has come.' He had had a dream the previous night – 23 September – in which Dalpat had ridden up to him and taken his leave: 'I have done as you wished,' he had said. Before Sir Pratap could recover and return to the regiment he was summoned back to India on the death of the young Maharaja Sumer Singh, who had been less than two years in power. Sir Pratap at once volunteered to take up the reins one more time as regent to the new ruler, HH Maharaja Umaid Singh. Charles

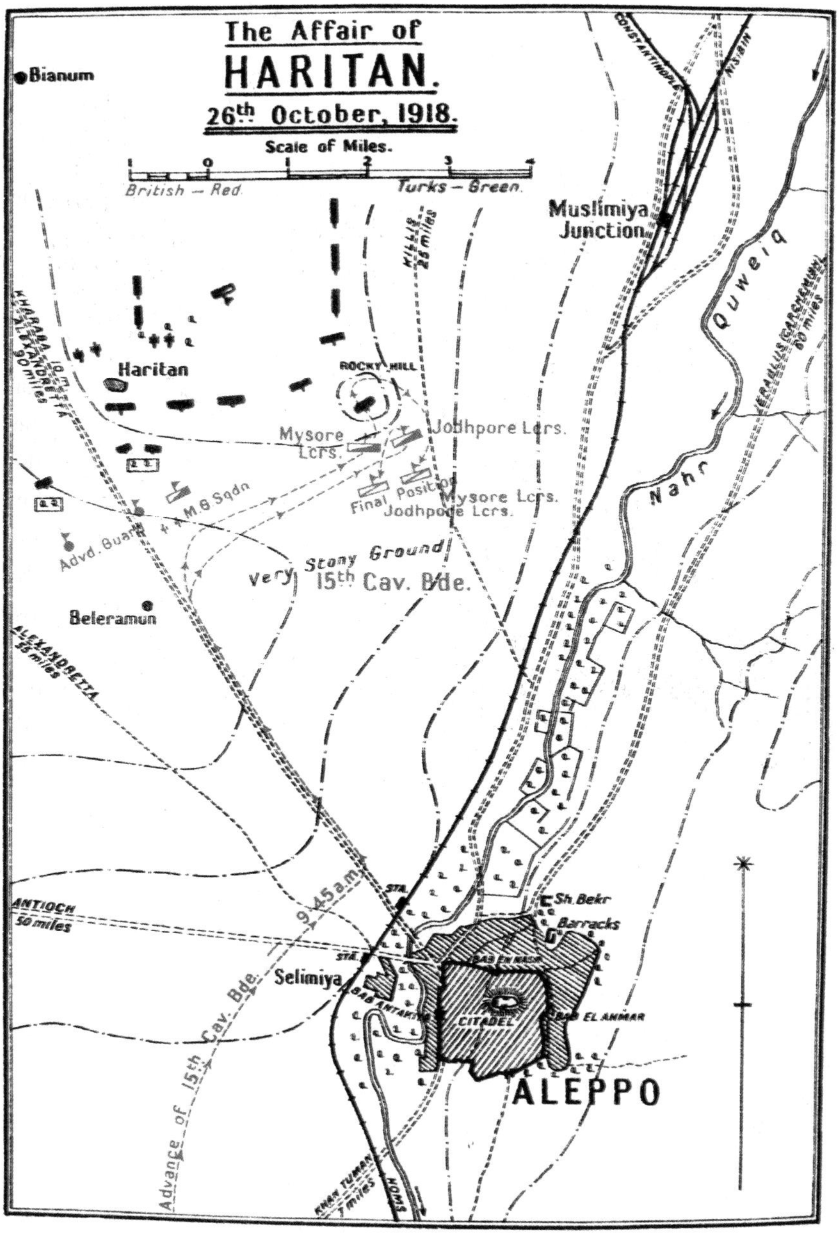

Map showing the Battle of Haritan.

Hervey wrote: 'His departure was a tremendous loss to the Brigade. While he was with us there was never a murmur or complaint from the Jodhpur Lancers. He ruled them with a rod of iron and every order from the Brigade had to be carried out to the letter. He used to say to the General "What you order, I and the Jodhpur Lancers obey – Jo Hukum."'

Sir Pratap was briefly ill in 1920 and, expecting to die, insisted on being dressed in his uniform and sword. Fortunately he recovered but died suddenly on 10 September 1922. His ashes were interred, at his request, near the polo ground in Jodhpur so that the dust from his beloved horses' hooves could still blow over him. Sadly, one of his four sons, Sagat Singh, who had won a Military Cross in Palestine, developed lung disease and died at an early age. As a memorial to Sir Pratap, scholarships were set up in his name at Sandhurst and at the Indian Military Academy at Dehra Dun for young Indian cadets.

After the glorious high points of Haifa and Henu, the Jodhpurs' last engagement of the war was to come as something of an anticlimax. A halt on 24 and 25 September gave the horses and the men a much-needed rest. On 26 September, the Hyderabad Lancers rejoined the Brigade, which then marched steadily northwards for several days, arriving just outside Damascus on 1 October, where they rested again for two days before resuming their advance. On 7 October Colonel Holden, the senior British officer serving with the Jodhpurs, entered Beirut with a detachment of armoured cars. On 2 October the Brigade was ordered to occupy a position astride the Aleppo-Alexandretta road, covering Aleppo from the north-west and, on the way, to clear a ridge west of Aleppo which was reported as occupied by the enemy. No enemy were found on the ridge; they had evacuated the town itself. At about 11.00 a.m. the Brigade moved north-west from Aleppo along the road to Alexandretta. About seven miles from Aleppo, as they reached the crest of a ridge, the advanced guard – consisting of two squadrons of Jodhpurs and a subsection of the machine gun squadron – came under heavy fire from the vicinity of the village of Haritan. The advance guard immediately took up a firing position along the ridge, with 'B' Squadron on the right of 'A' Squadron.

The brigadier decided that instant action was called for. The Mysore Lancers were therefore ordered to move round the east of the ridge and to charge the enemy position with the remaining two squadrons of Jodhpurs following up in support. At noon, the Lancers charged with great dash, in the face of artillery and rifle fire, and carried a position held by some 150 Turks. However, it was then found that the enemy, with over 2,000 Turkish and German troops with eight guns, was in far greater strength than had been realized. The Mysores fell back and rallied to the rear, with the Jodhpurs extending the line to the left. Unfortunately, as Colonel Holden went forward to reconnoitre the ground, he was killed by machine gun fire. The enemy advanced as if to counter-attack but dug in and retired after dark. So ended the Jodhpur Lancers' last battle of the war. On 27 October, they were relieved and went into bivouac near Aleppo. The armistice with Turkey came into force on the 31st. Between 19 September and 26 October the Jodhpur Lancers had marched over 500 miles. They remained in the Middle East as part of the Army of Occupation until November 1919 and returned to Jodhpur in February 1920. During the four years of the war, three Indian officers had been killed in action, one died of wounds, one of disease and twelve were wounded. Twenty-five NCOs and men were killed in action, six died of wounds, sixty-three died of disease and eighty-two were wounded. Two British officers were killed in action while serving with the regiment and two were wounded.

After the war was over, myths and legends grew around the great fight at Haifa but these cannot compare with the stark reality of victory. Two superb bronze cannon, captured at Haifa and brought back in triumph to Jodhpur, now stand outside the entrance to the royal retreat at Sardar Samand. The cast lettering reveals that these were made at Mechelen, in what is now Belgium, in 1578 by the famous gun-maker Gerard Nieuwenhuysen. Gerard had succeeded Remigny de Halut – to whom he was related by marriage – as master founder. The arms on the cannon, according to Burke's *General Armory*, are those of the Martin family (Gules a chevron between in chief three martlets and in base a crescent argent). A Turkish inscription had also been scratched into the barrels at some stage. How and when the cannon travelled from Belgium to Haifa remains a mystery. Whatever their history, the cannon have made a long journey from Europe to India and serve as a fine memorial to a great day in the Lancers' history. Another memorial is the Teen Murti (Three Statues) memorial in Delhi. It was built in 1922 to commemorate Indian soldiers from three princely states, including Jodhpur State, Hyderabad State and Mysore State. This memorial reminds passers-by of the great achievements of the 15th (Imperial Service)

Cannon captured at Haifa at Sardar Samand Palace, the maharaja's country retreat.

The names of almost 4,000 Indian soldiers, including Jodhpur Lancers, killed in action during the Egypt and Palestine Campaigns in 1918, are recorded at the Heliopolis Memorial near Cairo.

Cavalry Brigade, recording the Brigade's battle honours and honouring the names of those who lost their lives. The life-size bronze statue of the Jodhpur Lancer sergeant, with its unblinking gaze, symbolizes the uncompromising and inflexible pride of a Rathore as it looks over the present-day traffic that swirls around the roundabout all day.

It would be very hard to imagine what it must have been like to face a cavalry charge in its full strength. Not many are left alive today who have seen or taken part in such an attack. As the official history of the Palestine campaign records: 'When the squadrons drove in spurs and thundered forward, with the sun glinting upon swords and lance-heads, the moral effect was overwhelming.'

Many of those who were privileged to take part in the last great victorious cavalry charge were the descendants of men who had fought at Khanua, Sumel, Dharmat, Merta and Malpura – some of the legendary Rathore charges.

KILLED IN ACTION
H N HOLDEN D.S.O
JEM ASSU SINGH I.O.M
JEM KHANG SINGH I.O.M
DAF MAN SINGH
DAF KOOM SINGH
LCE DAF REWAT SINGH
LCE DAF KHET SINGH
SR AZAM KHAN
SR HUSSEIN KHAN
SR BHOOR SINGH
SR KHANDOO SINGH
SR AMAN SINGH
SR PANEY SINGH
SR BALOO SINGH
SR TAGAT SINGH
SR SHAZAD SINGH
SR JUNJAR SINGH
DIED OF WOUNDS
MAJOR THAKUR DALPAT SINGH M.C.
TRUMP MAJ SHER SINGH I.O.M
DAF DHONKAL SINGH
SR GOPAL SINGH
SR SULTAN SINGH
MISSING
LCE DAF BHIR SINGH
SR LADHOO KHAN
SR MUSHARAF KHAN
SR KAN SINGH
SR DOOL SINGH
JODHPUR
LANCERS
THEIR NAME
LIVETH
FOR
EVERMORE

Chapter 6

INTERLUDE: 1918-39

The end of the Great War brought a return to what at least one officer termed 'proper soldiering' – the ceaseless round of drills, parades, exercises and, of course, polo. After the stresses of the previous four years, it was certainly a return to a more relaxed way of life. Lord Ismay, who was commissioned into the 21st PAVO Cavalry (the Daly's Horse), records that prior to the First World War, 'Sometimes there was a little office work to be done; sometimes we had a rifle inspection or a kit inspection or an inspection of saddlery; sometimes either a British officer or an Indian officer gave a short lecture on a variety of topics such as horse management or musketry. By lunchtime the day's work was over.' He was able to play polo three afternoons a week and to school ponies on the other days. However, the end of the War also brought with it the realization that the days of cavalrymen charging stirrup to stirrup were over. Slowly, remorselessly, the horse was to be replaced by the armoured car or the tank. In the Indian Army, as well as in the British Army, once proud regimental names began to disappear as amalgamations took place in order to reduce the number of cavalry regiments.

Maharaja Umaid Singh succeeded his elder brother Sumer Singh, who died in 1918. Born in 1903, the former had been educated at Mayo College and was

Facing Page: Teen Murti, New Delhi: The memorial to the 15th (Imperial Service) Cavalry Brigade.

HH Maharaja Umaid Singh in the uniform of the Jodhpur Lancers. He zealously fought red tape to get his regiment active action.

invested with full powers by the viceroy, Lord Reading, in 1923. He inherited a progressive kingdom with an efficient administration and in 1947 he bequeathed to India a model state with the beginnings of a representative government. He himself was a keen flyer, being one of India's first licensed pilots, and he developed Jodhpur as an international airport. In 1925 he led an all-conquering polo team to England. However, the maharaja was no pleasure-loving playboy. In order to provide work for his people at a time of great famine he ordered the building of the last of India's great palaces – the Umaid Bhawan.

The Lancers provided escorts for the visits of Viceroys Hardinge and Linlithgow to Jodhpur. It should not be thought that mounting ceremonial parades was an easy or routine affair. A file surviving in the archives of the Mehrangarh Fort details the arrangements for the viceroy's visit in 1916 and gives some insight into the effort and commitment that went into it. The viceroy

Major General R.C. Duncan, commandant, Jodhpur State Forces during the Second World War. Formerly a Gurkha officer, he later wrote the History of the Jodhpur State Forces 1939–45.

was to be met on the station platform by a guard of honour drawn from the 1st Risala under the command of Thakur Kishon Singh, and consisting of four officers with a hundred men and the Jaipur State Band. Outside the station there were to be another eighty men of the 2nd Risala under M.K. Inder Singh and Kanwar Gulab Singh, the commanding officer of the Jodhpur Infantry. The viceroy's route to the Residency was lined by men of the Jodhpur Infantry and the Camel Corps, with the infantrymen spaced ten paces apart and the Camel Corps mounted at fifteen paces. Every fifty yards there was an officer or NCO and at the Residency Gate there were forty men of the 2nd Risala. Immediately outside the Residency there was another guard of honour under the command of Subedar Jawan Singh, consisting of three officers, a hundred men, the Lancer colour party (consisting of the regimental standard carried by a senior non-commissioned officer or an officer and escorted by a small group of

The Umaid Bhawan Palace, Jodhpur, under construction.

Lord Rawlinson's visit to Jodhpur in 1923.

senior NCOs) and the Jodhpur State Band. Throughout the viceroy's time in the city there was a bodyguard stationed at the Residency, consisting of one officer and twenty-nine other ranks of the 1st Risala. In all, well over 500 troops were on parade. The State Band was obviously a matter of some pride; in 1929 this consisted of forty-four musicians under the command of bandmaster Captain Ryman and was reported to be 'A really excellent band; difficult to beat and a pleasure to listen to!'

In the Royal Archives at Windsor there is a report on Lord Rawlinson's visit to Jodhpur in April 1923. He was then commander-in-chief, India. 'Immediately on our arrival I inspected the five squadrons of the Jodhpur Lancers. I was quite delighted with them. They have three service squadrons, a headquarters squadron and a reserve squadron which is a better organisation than that previously adopted of two regiments of three squadrons with nothing behind them. The experience of the War, in which the Jodhpur Lancers won a high reputation for valour and discipline, has taught them the necessity of a reserve organisation ready to keep them up to strength, both in men and horses, when they proceed on service. They drilled well and the gallop past was highly creditable. These Rathores are natural horsemen, born in the saddle, and very keen on soldiering.'

Lord Rawlinson had accompanied Lord Roberts to a state banquet in Jodhpur in 1889 at which the latter had said that he was sure that the newly formed Jodhpur Lancers would maintain the tradition of their Rathore ancestors. 'I was able to quote this in my speech and say that his [Lord Robert's] prophecy had been more than fulfilled by the high reputation which the Jodhpur Lancers had earned during the Great War, both in France and in Palestine, and that it is not too much to say that this body of horse is certainly one of the best cavalry regiments, if not the best, maintained by an Indian State.'

The Annual Report on the Imperial Service Forces for 1922–23 comments on the regiment as follows: 'The Jodhpur Lancers are commanded by Lt-Colonel Thakur Pratap Singh, Sardar Bahadur CBE, an old but gallant Commanding Officer who has much influence with his men and who commands considerable respect. The officers and men are of that fine fighting class of Rathore Rajputs. Excellent recruits are forthcoming. The unit is excellently mounted on small walers in good condition. Training throughout the year has been systematic and thorough. Equipment is complete and well kept. Interior economy is good,

Drilling and marching did not come naturally to the new 'native' regiments unused to the discipline of modern British units. These were lessons learned 'day in and day out'; and what better occasion than to welcome a dignitary!

the men are well paid and contented and discipline is reported good. Lines and barracks are all that can be desired. The regiment is fit for service.'

Lieutenant Colonel Thakur Pratap Singh had retired in 1925 at the age of sixty-two, after forty-one years of service with the unit; eighteen of them in command. He had joined as a squadron leader in 1894, had taken part in the expedition to China and represented the Jodhpur Lancers at the coronation of King George V in London in 1911. He commanded the Lancers during the Great War and was granted a King's Commission besides being awarded the Order of British India (First Class) and the CBE. While in command he introduced a new

training curriculum which improved the horsemanship within the regiment to the extent that other princely states would send their men to Jodhpur for training. On his retirement, Maharaja Umaid Singh wrote of him: 'He has shown loyalty, devotion to duty and the highest qualities of a soldier, whether in service or on the field. It is not too much to say that the efficiency of the Sardar Risala during the Great War and after, is to a great extent due to the influence of Colonel Thakur Pratap Singh.'

In 1922 Amar Singh, by now a lieutenant colonel, was appointed to command the newly formed Jaipur Lancers. He noted in his diary that the Jodhpur Lancers

Sir Pratap and his men did not quite care for the ceremonial part of soldiering, but it was very much a part of the duties before and, indeed, through the Wars.

were the standard to aim at and that they were recognized as the best unit amongst the Rajasthan cavalry and were probably the best cavalry unit in the whole of the State Forces. An intense but friendly rivalry, both in terms of military prowess and on the polo ground, quickly grew between the two regiments and their respective commanders Amar Singh and Colonel Dalpat Singh. In 1930 the Jaipur Lancers were inspected by the Maharajas of Jaipur and Jodhpur and the latter complimented Amar Singh on the standard of horsemanship in his regiment.

The Annual Report for 1924–25 describes the Jodhpur Lancers as 'very fine fighting material, chiefly Rathore Rajputs of the Jodhpur State and very well mounted on an excellent stamp of Waler. A well turned-out unit which has

undergone a systematic course of training throughout the past year; very good in the field.' The following year's report comments: 'This State does it troops very well. They are happy and contented and efficient. His Highness Umaid Singh takes a personal interest in them and it is a pleasure to see him and his staff on the occasion of the Annual Sports taking part in judging and competing.'

The Annual Report in 1929–30 included the following comments: 'Lt-Colonel Rai Bahadur Thakur Dalpat Singh has recently taken over command and should do well. He has attended Sargor (the Equitation School) and Pachmari (the Musketry School) and been attached to the 34th PAVO Cavalry. The officers are young men of a very good type; some of the Squadron Commanders are on the old side. The regiment is very well horsed; the turn-out of men and horses is excellent. Riding is excellent and there are very good barracks. Progress in training is satisfactory except that the officers show a lack of tactical knowledge. A fine spirit prevails in the regiment.' The report for the following year noted: 'The majority of the officers are experienced and capable. The cadet commissioned officers are promising.' A recurring complaint in these reports is about the lack of proper training facilities for the officers of the Imperial Service Forces. Three-month courses for senior officers were held at Jaipur in 1928, at Gwalior in 1929 and at Hyderabad in 1932. Starting 1932, twenty places were reserved for cadets from the State Forces at the Indian Military Academy at Dehra Dun.

Central to the regiment's sporting activities between the wars was, of course, polo! A year before Sir Pratap's death, the then Prince of Wales, later King Edward VIII, visited Jodhpur. The prince himself being a keen polo player, a tournament was arranged in his honour. It was in the final of this tournament that Jodhpur beat the hitherto unbeaten Patiala. Sir Pratap, who was watching in the stand, remained absolutely motionless throughout the play, even when Jodhpur scored their winning last-minute goal. When the horn sounded, indicating the end of play, the old man, now seventy-seven, stood up with tears pouring down his cheeks. The winning team included Colonel Hanut Singh and two future commanding officers of the Lancers: Thakur Prithi Singh and Thakur Dalpat Singh. Sadly, Colonel Thakur Prithi Singh, a grandson of Sir Pratap – his mother was a daughter of Sir Pratap – died while playing polo in 1936.

However, it should not be thought that during these years of peace, the regiment neglected its military skills. Major Hem Singh was 9th out of 251 competitors in the King's Medal Rifle Shoot in 1930 with a score of 292. He came second in the Imperial Service Forces Championship and second also in the competition for entrants from the mounted branch. Subedar Major Bahadur Singh of the Jodhpur Infantry was fourth in the ISF Championship. During the winters of 1937 and 1938 the Lancers carried out regimental and brigade training with the Meerut Cavalry Brigade. This was a private arrangement – approved by Maharaja Umaid Singh – between Brigadier Duncan, commanding the Jodhpur State Forces, and Brigadier J. Lumley, commanding the Meerut Cavalry Brigade. The cost of these exercises, some Rs 3,600 each year, was borne by the state of Jodhpur. These few weeks of training with other units were invaluable. In 1935 the military-adviser-in-chief's Annual Review of State Forces stated that the Jodhpur Lancers were a very good cavalry regiment with fine traditions from

Polo remained very much a part of the Jodhpur Lancers right up to mechanization; with several of the regiment's commanding officers like Thakur Prithi Singh Bera (fourth from left) and Thakur Dalpat Singh Rohet in the front rank of India's finest players. Rao Raja Hanut Singh (first left), the Jodhpur Lancer's youngest ever officer (fourteen years in 1914), was arguably the country's greatest polo player.

the Great War. A couple of years later, referring to the training with the Meerut Brigade, he commented that the regiment 'derived great benefit from it. The material is excellent.' It is possible that comments like these led to the selection of the Jodhpur Lancers for active service in the Second World War.

Chapter 7

THE SECOND WORLD WAR

The Second World War was a truly global war in a way that even the First World War had not been, with India itself being threatened with invasion by the Japanese incursion into neighbouring Burma. By 1945 two million Indians were under arms – the largest wholly volunteer army the world has ever seen. The number enrolled in the State Forces had increased tenfold, from 4,829 in 1940 to 41,463 in 1945. Indian troops fought in the deserts of North Africa, the mountains of Italy and the jungles of Arakan, Burma and Malaya. One-sixth of all the Victoria Crosses awarded in the Second World War went to Indian soldiers. However, the Jodhpur Lancers, through no fault of their own, were to play little part in these significant events.

The then ruler, Maharaja Umaid Singh – convinced that war with Germany was inevitable – sent a telegram to the viceroy, Lord Linlithgow, on 17 September 1938: 'In view of the grave international situation, I feel it my duty to request Your Excellency kindly to communicate to HM the King Emperor an expression of my unflinching loyalty to His Person and throne at this crisis. I beg further to offer my personal services unreservedly and to place all the resources of my State, both Civil and Military, at the disposal of the Imperial Government in the event

Facing page: Cannon at the Mehrangarh Fort.

of war breaking out.' However, such loyalty to the British Government was to receive scant recognition in 1947.

The viceroy, on a state visit to Jodhpur in 1939, in a speech said: 'Your Highness was among the first last autumn when a crisis developed which led to the immediate threat of war, to offer the assistance of all the resources of the State; and I feel no shadow of doubt that should the need arise, amongst the foremost to the help of the Empire will be Your Highness and the State of Jodhpur.' At that time the Jodhpur State Forces consisted of the Lancers together with a training squadron, an infantry regiment, a mule supply train, a field hospital and the Palace Guard – a total of some 1,700 men. By the end of the war this number was to be increased fourfold. The maharaja himself was commander-in-chief and the commandant Brigadier R.C. Duncan MVO OBE. The three British officers attached to the Lancers at this time were:

Lieutenant Colonel G.G. Collyns	3rd Cavalry
Captain A.G.S. Alexander	Central India Horse
Captain G.D.G. Garforth Bles	Guides Cavalry

The advent of the Second World War saw a significant increase in the number of State troops. Bikaner, for instance, raised two additional infantry battalions in addition to infantry and artillery training centres. In Gwalior, the existing lancer and infantry regiments were brought up to full strength. Two more infantry battalions were raised and infantry, artillery and divisional reconnaissance centres were founded. During the years 1939–45 the Jodhpur State Army expanded to about four times its original pre-war strength; an expansion as great, if not greater than that of any other Indian State Forces. Two new infantry battalions were raised together with the Jodhpur Bodyguard Squadron. Training centres were set up for both the Lancers and the infantry, and the Jodhpur General Purposes Transport Company was formed.

If the Jodhpur Lancers were frustrated in France between 1914 and 1917, it was nothing compared to the frustration they were to suffer in the Second World War. Initially the regiment was chosen as the only state regiment, together with the Probyn's Horse, the 11th (Prince Albert Victor's Own) Cavalry and the Royal Deccan Horse, to continue as a mounted regiment. However, it soon became clear that the days of cavalry charges were over, and in 1941 they exchanged their

Maharaja Umaid Singh (sixth from left) with Jodhpur Lancers in Palestine during the Second World War.

horses for armoured cars and became a Divisional Reconnaissance Regiment. Unfortunately, however, when their division, the 25th Indian, left India for Burma, the area was considered to be unsuitable terrain for such vehicles and the Lancers ended up in the Middle East without ever firing a shot in anger. This in spite of the fact that they were the first State Force to serve with the Crown Forces and also the first such regiment selected for mechanization. However, by a happy chance, the Jodhpur Infantry Regiment, which had not expected to see service outside the state, were to see action and to add to the state's military reputation – being the first Indian troops to land on the mainland of Italy at Salerno in 1944.

In September 1939 the Lancers commenced intensive training at Surpura, some six miles from Jodhpur, where they were visited by the maharaja. In keeping with the hectic nature of the times, and to their intense disappointment, they returned to Jodhpur after only one month. However, in January 1940 the regiment left, on six special trains, for Risalpur on the North-West Frontier under the command of Lieutenant Colonel Thakur Bahadur Singh OBI. During the

Maharaja Umaid Singh (top left) and his younger brother, Ajit Singh, inspecting a Jodhpur Lancer armoured car in the Middle East during the Second World War.

journey it was found that the father of one of the subalterns had stowed away on the train as it left Jodhpur; he remained, for some time, as an honorary member of the regiment! At this time the strength of the regiment was: seventeen state officers, two state officer cadets, twenty-one Indian officers, 468 Indian other ranks, 383 followers and 521 horses. The regiment remained at Risalpur for about eighteen months. (See Appendix 3 for full list of the officers at this time.) The training squadron which remained at Jodhpur under the command of Captain Thakur Zabar Singh, with Lieutenant Mangal Singh as adjutant, comprised five Indian officers, 134 Indian other ranks, ten followers and 134 horses. The role of this squadron was to provide initial training for recruits to the regiment.

In February 1941 the regiment was informed that it had been selected for mechanization. Instead of looking after a horse they had to now drive and maintain a motor vehicle. During the months of March and April, officers and NCOs were attached to either the Royal Deccan Horse at Mardan or the 13th Lancers at Risalpur for short courses on driving and maintenance; some sowars were attached to either the 8th Cavalry at Kohat or the 19th Lancers at Sialkot

Field Marshal Auchinleck, commander-in-chief, India, visiting the Jodhpur State Forces Training Centre in Jodhpur during the Second World War.

for the same purpose. Equipment was in very short supply – the Probyn's Horse did not receive their first (and for a time, only) tank until April 1941. The Jo Hokums received thirty-five lorries in May and the regiment settled down to training in earnest. In July Lieutenant Colonel G.G. Collyns took over command from Lieutenant Colonel Bahadur Singh, who had completed the full term of his command and had gone on leave pending his retirement. Captain Garforth-Bles left for the Indian Armoured Corps Training Centre and was replaced by Captain J.B. Hampdon of the 10th/12th Frontier Force Regiment. In July the regiment was inspected by General Sir Archibald Wavell, the newly appointed commander-in-chief and later viceroy.

During February the regiment undertook a range of inter-squadron and inter-regimental exercises with the Probyn's Horse. In March the regiment joined a 1st Cavalry Brigade training march, during which river crossings and night operations were practised. In order not to give away their position by coughing when on patrol, every man in the regiment volunteered to give up smoking, with the exception of the farrier dafadar. The Northern Command arranged anti-aircraft exercises in July in which the regiment took part, while the officers took part in Brigade reconnaissances of the Mohmand and Utman Khel area. As the other cavalry regiments from the Indian Army were being mechanized, there were many surplus horses. The Jodhpurs received specially selected horses from the Probyn's Horse, the Skinner's Horse and the 16th/5th Lancers, so that the regiment was splendidly mounted. The polo ponies were put into strict training as there were several good polo grounds at Risalpur and plenty of competition from other regiments in the area. The Jodhpur Lancers maintained their high standard, winning many tournaments at Risalpur and Peshawar during this period. In the following year they won the Mardan Tournament as well as the Peshawar Christmas Tournament. They were greatly helped by coaching from Maharaj Kishen Singh, who had been a famous polo player and was the father of Lieutenant Prem Singh. Sadly, at the end of 1941, the ponies had to be returned to Jodhpur because of the forthcoming restrictions on the movement of animals by rail due to other demands on the transport system.

While the Lancers were proud to be selected for mechanization, there was sadness that they would lose their much-loved horses. A Rajput's love for his horse was an accepted fact, and with the horses would go much of the regiment's tradition, and needless to mention – polo! Hence, a mounted bodyguard was raised in 1941 from pensioners or men who were close to pension and who wished to remain with their beloved horses. Their role was to act as Palace Guards and to give aid to the civil power if necessary. Because there was a considerable surplus of horses within the Indian Army at this time, the bodyguard was able to take their pick of the mounts available – and those selected included the polo ponies. The bodyguard consisted of three troops of Rajputs and one of Kaimkhanis, and was commanded by Captain Mangal Singh of the Lancers Training Centre. The majority of the men came from the Jodhpur Lancers but there was a small proportion from regular Indian Army regiments, recruited from within Jodhpur. Risaldar Baxu Khan of the bodyguard was awarded the Order of British India (Second Class) in 1946. The bodyguard had been renamed the Durga Horse in 1945, and in 1951 was merged with the Kachwara Horse from Jaipur. In 1953, these became part of the 61st Cavalry, India's only mounted regiment to maintain the traditions of the Jodhpur Lancers, including the annual Haifa Day celebrations.

The Jodhpur Lancers Training Centre was responsible for training recruits for the regiment, and at the outbreak of the war was commanded by Captain Thakur Zabar Singh, a grandson of Sir Pratap. Mechanization demanded changes here too as a new organization had to be built up from scratch. Many recruits had only a very basic education and had to be taught to meet the challenges of their new technical role. Suitable garages and workshops had to be built and there was shortage of instructors and equipment; for instance, it wasn't until 1943 that the first wireless sets were received. In spite of all these difficulties, by 1944 the training centre was the largest in India with over a thousand officers and men on roll at any one time. Not only was it the largest but also the best training centre, according to Brigadier Inskip, the deputy military adviser-in-chief to State Forces. Major Thakur Zabar Singh was awarded a well-deserved MBE in 1943 for his work at the centre.

It was on 20 October 1941 that the Jodhpur Lancers left for Bolarum, Secunderabad – a five-day journey – to join the 18th (later re-numbered 19th) Indian Division as its Divisional Reconnaissance Regiment. At this time the Division was commanded by Major General Smyth VC MC, who lost no time in getting to know the officers and men both on and off parade. The war establishment of a Divisional Reconnaissance Regiment was a regimental headquarters and four squadrons. The Headquarters Squadron included a mortar troop, a signals troop and a Light Aid Detachment for vehicle recovery

Maharaja Umaid Singh (seated centre on a chair) with officers of the Jodhpur Lancers during the Second World War.

and repair, as well as those concerned with the regiment's administration. The three 'Sabre' squadrons included a squadron headquarters, four armoured carrier troops and a rifle troop, the carrier troops being mounted in Bren carriers and the rifle troop in 15-cwt trucks. Later, armoured cars replaced the carriers in one troop. Vehicles and weapons were slow in arriving at the regiment, which meant that in exercises with the infantry brigades of the Division it was only

possible to put one squadron into the field at a time. After eight months spent training at Bolarum, the regiment moved further south and joined the 2nd Indian Division, based first at Attur and later at Chinna Salem.

A report that a Japanese invasion fleet was heading for Madras, together with air-raids along the south coast, caused consternation. Two squadrons of the regiment were hurriedly sent to the east coast on coast-watching duty between

Cuddalore and Dhaneskhodi. A third squadron was sent to Trichinopoly. Their War Diary sets out the role of the Lancers as: 'To ascertain and report any landings between the Coleroon and Ponnaiyar rivers, to maintain touch with the enemy and report their strength. To delay any advance towards Trinchinopoly as long as possible.' Unfortunately, because of the shortage of vehicles, only Major Sultan Singh – acting as a liaison officer at divisional headquarters – and three carriers and their crews as the divisional commander's personal escort were able to accompany the Division. In any event, it turned out to be a false alarm, although two Japanese aircrafts did bomb Coconada. Shortly afterwards, the regiment came under the command of the 20th Indian Division and was to be sent further south to the Attur area, except for one squadron, which was bound for Trichinopoly. Before the move was completed it was decided that the regiment would come under the command of headquarters, Madras District. Finally, in August 1942, the regiment became Divisional Reconnaissance Regiment to the 25th Indian Division. At last it was fully equipped with anti-tank rifles and Bren guns as well as with more armoured carriers. It carried out a series of anti-invasion patrols along the coast, which unfortunately prevented training at a regimental level and also wore out the tyres of the vehicles very quickly; replacements were hard to come by so vehicles were immobilized for lack of tyres.

At the end of November 1942, the regiment took part in Exercise Minx, a divisional exercise designed to test its war role in the case of invasion. The plan was that the Division would concentrate around Trichinopoly, covered by the Lancers, who would report on any landing by the Japanese and delay their advance as far as possible. As far as the Jodhpurs were concerned, the exercise was literally a wash-out as it rained for five days and there was no sign of the 'enemy'. During the month of December, vehicles from the regiment took part in a 'motor show' organized by the 74th Indian Infantry Brigade, winning the classes for camouflaged three-tonners and the Towing Class, also for three-tonners. In March the following year the regiment took part in Exercise Trump in which the 19th and 25th Divisions were opposed to one another. The Lancers were described by one officer as 'the best thing there' and gave a good account of themselves when pitted against the 19th Lancers in the initial advance-to-contact phase of the exercise. In May, Major W.W.A. Loring took over command of the regiment with Major Shyam Singh as second-in-command. Captain Dhonkal Singh was adjutant and the squadron commanders were Majors Kalyan Singh,

Arjun Singh and Chandan Singh. At the same time the old and worn out Marmon Harrington armoured cars were replaced by Humber Armoured Car Mark IIIs and Daimlers.

Major Loring instituted a vigorous training programme, including early morning physical training for all officers, which he himself attended. Battle craft was taught through a number of exercises supervised with much realism and enthusiasm by Major Chandan Singh and Captain Mohan Singh, who had themselves recently returned from a battle training course. By June, therefore, the regiment was ready to take part in a major exercise – Exercise Fog – arranged for thirty-three corps. The initial tasks alloted to the regiment were to reconnoitre widely on the right flank of the 25th Division, while at the same time providing one squadron to act as a mobile advance guard to the leading elements of the 55th Brigade. These two tasks together were really too big to be undertaken by one regiment. Nevertheless, the Lancers did well, gathering information and confusing the 'enemy'. During the 'withdrawal' phase of the exercise, the regiment 'captured' the second-in-command and adjutant of their opposite numbers, the Hyderabad Lancers, and following one particularly successful action, Major Kalyan Singh was deemed by an umpire to have 'won a DSO'. However, on the final day of this phase, when the Lancers were covering a key village named Mulbagal, disaster struck. The commanding officer, returning from a conference at divisional headquarters was informed that the Hyderabad Lancers, together with an infantry brigade, had somehow got behind the Jodhpurs and entered Mulbagal. Only swift and aggressive action by 'B' and 'C' Squadrons together with a counter-attack led by the Signals Officer Captain Ramdan Singh, saved the situation. Afterwards, whenever things were particularly difficult, the divisional staff referred to it as being a 'proper Mulbagal'. At the end of the exercise, the regiment was congratulated by the divisional commander on its magnificently aggressive spirit.

The Burma Campaign of 1942 taught the Indian Army the importance of special training in jungle warfare, and by July the Division had been ordered to train in these tactics despite there being hardly any rugged forest terrain in their area. In August the regiment took part in another corps exercise – Trump II. Amongst the highlights of this exercise was the commanding officer being 'killed' on the first afternoon, only to be brought back to life one and a half hours later, and a bridge being 'blown' while 'B' Squadron were still on the far side.

Jodhpur's contribution to the defence of India continued after the Second World War with Rao Raja Narpat Singh (sitting extreme right), Sir Pratap's eldest son on the committee, set up to found the National War Academy, 1946.

Sitting: Sir Mirza Ismail, Dr Amarnath Jha, H.E. Field Marshal Sir Claude Auchinleck, Lieutenant General Sir Arthur Smith, R.B. Rao Raja Narpat Singh. Standing: Brigadier S.P.P. Thorat, Vice Admiral Sir Geoffrey Miles, K.B. Mian Afzal Hussain, G.S. Bhalla, Air Marshal H.S.P. Walmsley, A.E. Foot, Dr D.M. Sen.

This squadron later took part in a spirited action against the 70th Divisional Reconnaissance Regiment while Lieutenant Prem Singh spent four days 'out in the blue' controlling patrols. The regiment's successes in these major exercises were to make the subsequent decision not to employ them in Burma all the more difficult to bear.

October and November were very difficult months for the regiment. Their campsite was badly flooded, necessitating the stripping down of a large number of vehicles before they could be used again. Unfortunately the technical officer, Captain Cooper, whose advice and assistance would have been invaluable at a time like this, had come down with pneumonia. Major Hanmer too was very ill during this period and was away from the regiment for two months. In December the regiment moved into the Mysore Jungle and 'B' Squadron took part in a divisional exercise as part of the 'enemy' force. It quickly became clear how difficult it was for armoured cars to operate on the narrow tracks through the jungle. Therefore, in January 1944 when the regiment was engaged in another divisional exercise, patrolling was carried out on foot or in carriers. However, when in February the 25th Division was ordered to the Arakan to meet a strong Japanese attack, it was decided that the Lancers should not go with them as there would be little opportunity for the deployment of armoured cars in the jungle. After all their hard work and training, this came.

Maharaja Umaid Singh demanded that the Lancers be deployed in a more active role. He had planned to visit the regiment in February but this had to be postponed at very short notice due to another invasion scare, which too turned out to be a false alarm. However, perhaps because of his intervention, the regiment was warned in March that it was to go to the Middle East as part of PAIFORCE (Persia and Iraq Command), which was responsible for defending the vital oilfields in Iraq, where there had been an anti-British uprising in 1941. As many men as possible were given leave and on 1 May 1944 the regiment, now commanded by Lieutenant Colonel Hanmer, arrived at a transit camp in Bombay. They sailed on the *SS Ekma*, without their vehicles, on 12 May, arriving at Basra in Persia (now Iraq) on 19 May, where they stayed for two weeks for acclimatization. Those who were there still remember how, during the voyage, the men erected a shrine in one of the ship's holds to conduct a purifying ritual with fire in the name of the mother goddess. The ship's captain was, not surprisingly, concerned about the risk of the fire spreading and ordered the fires to be extinguished. Shortly afterwards there was a tremendous storm. The Lancers immediately pointed out that this was entirely the captain's fault and that the gods were angry because the fires had been put out. The captain agreed to the re-lighting of the fires provided there was a fire picquet on guard, and went so far as to place his own cap by the shrine.

On their arrival at Basra, the Jodhpurs re-equipped with Humber Armoured Cars Marks III and IV, together with armoured carriers and white scout cars. Later they were also to receive Staghound armoured cars equipped for an anti-aircraft role. The regiment was ordered to relieve the Poona Horse, who had been their comrades in the Secunderabad Brigade in 1914, and who were now guarding the Anglo-Iranian oilfields. The handover between the Poona Horse and the Jodhpur Lancers proved to be a happy reunion for the Rajputs and Kayamkhanies in each regiment as the Poona Horse recruited the majority of their men from the state of Jodhpur. The Maharaja of Jodhpur was an honorary colonel of the Poona Horse and had raised two squadrons of Rathores for service in the regiment. The regiment was deployed by squadrons, with regimental headquarters at Hafkhel. The country was hilly with only a little vegetation in the valleys, and the roads were just a little wider than tracks. Such was the area to be covered that one of the squadrons was nearly 150 miles from HQ. The Jodhpurs were to spend five months guarding the oilfields, but two tragedies marred their stay. On 8 August, Major K. Surajbhan Singh was killed in an accident when his armoured car over-turned. Later that month, their Commanding Officer, Lieutenant Colonel R.G. Hanmer, was found to be suffering from infantile paralysis and was sent home to England. During August, a composite squadron, under the command of Major Chandan Singh, went on a long-range training drive which eventually was to cover 1,600 miles. The object of this exercise was to show the flag and also to allow the sowars to see parts of Persia not normally visited by British forces.

In November the Lancers handed over their responsibilities to the 10th Baluch Regiment and moved to Ahwaz. From there they went to join the 24th Indian Brigade at a camp which was being slowly, very slowly, constructed at Andimishk, where they arrived on 12 December. No sooner had they arrived than it started to rain heavily and the whole camp was turned into a quagmire. Only the most strenous efforts got things back into order for a five-day visit by the Maharaja at the end of the month. In the New Year 1945, the regiment got down to collective training, first at troop and then at the squadron level. In February, the squadrons were attached to infantry battalions and carried out exercises with them. 'A' Squadron was chosen to give a demonstration to the whole Brigade on how to clear a road block while 'C' Squadron and Regimental HQ went to take part in manoeuvres with the 27th Indian brigade. The regimental rifle team, consisting of one officer, two NCOs and five sowars won second place in the inter-regimental meet at Cairo. Jemadar Lal Singh was the best individual shot amongst the contestants from the Indian Army.

In March, the regiment – less 'C' Squadron and regimental headquarters – took part in Exercise Circus, a three-week long brigade exercise, where it acted as advance guard to the Brigade as well as undertook road protection, a tedious business which involved constant daylight patrols. The conduct of the regiment was described as exemplary, with march discipline, camouflage and blackout all being strictly observed. It then returned to the oilfields for a further, fairly uneventful six months, the monotony being broken by celebrations for Victory-in-Europe and Victory-in-Japan days. A regular supply of Indian films also helped to relieve the tedium. The only problem during this period was a series of thefts of telephone wire. Patrols were instigated in an attempt to prevent these thefts and escorts were also provided for the signalmen who went out to repair the damage. On 10 September 1945 a patrol from 'B' Squadron, under the command of Risaldar Partap Singh, was sent out following a report that the line had been cut again. Locating the break, a thorough search of the area was carried out and a bundle of wire, some food and a pair of shoes were found. A boy aged about twelve was also found in a nearby hut and he eventually led the party to a nearby village and identified two men as the thieves. The three were then handed over to the civil police and thefts in that area decreased significantly. Elsewhere, on another occasion, when a patrol was accompanying a signal repair party, three Persians were seen acting suspiciously. When challenged, one of them attacked Dafadar Sohan Singh with a dagger and in the ensuing struggle, one Persian was killed. The stolen wire was recovered and there were no further incidents of this kind.

On 25 October 1945, the regiment left Persia and moved to Haifa to relieve the Patiala Lancers and in order to protect the refinery and its associated pipeline through the Jordan Valley. It was perhaps nothing short of justice that after all their disappointments, the regiment should be given the opportunity to visit the site where their predecessors had earned such glory. Veterans recall that sadly, in spite of the most careful search, it proved impossible at that time to locate Dalpat Singh's grave, though more recently the grave has been re-located. The oil installations were under attack both from Arabs and Jews – the latter being especially troublesome. A series of daytime observation posts were set up along the length of the pipeline and there were regular patrols at dawn and dusk, this in addition to standing patrols at vulnerable points during the night. The Lancers made it clear to the Jewish settlers that they did not understand their language and would shoot anything that moved within twenty yards of the pipeline. The final duty of the regiment in the Middle East – under the command of Sir Pratap's grandson Captain Rao Raja Bijai Singh – was to escort a demoralized Vichy French Division from Syria to Tripoli in Lebanon, from where the French troops were returned to France.

Their task finished, the Lancers returned home in 1946 for a victory parade through the streets of Jodhpur, to a tumultuous welcome from the residents. In their formal welcome address, the citizens of Jodhpur included the following well-earned tribute to the officers and men of the regiment: 'Your exemplary conduct and character, your high sense of duty and discipline, your spirit of service and sacrifice, and above all your lofty spirit of unflinching loyalty to our beloved Master coupled with devotion to your Motherland, have been beyond all praise. These are virtues which people in other walks of life will do well to emulate, and which evoke our unstinted admiration and respect.'

The Sardar Infantry 1939–45

By a curious chance, even as the Lancers trained so hard for battle they were denied the opportunity to strike a blow against the enemy. The Jodhpur Sardar Infantry, who as an inexperienced infantry unit had not expected to see action, were to gain glory in Italy in a new role. In June 1941 they sailed from Karachi for Eritrea. In April 1942 they moved to Egypt, where they were assigned the mundane tasks of guarding a large base ordnance depot and a number of prisoner-of-war camps. During this largely uneventful stretch of time, an enterprising German officer tried to escape in a British battledress, wearing a monocle and pretending to be Lieutenant Colonel Rogers – the commanding officer of the Jodhpur Infantry. His disguise was good, he even spoke a little Urdu, but as luck would have it he chose to try a gate seldom used by the CO.

The NCO of the guard became suspicious and arrested him. By New Year 1943, the battalion had almost lost hope of ever getting a change from its static role, and the future seemed depressing and dreary.

In May, however, their fortunes changed dramatically. They were chosen to form the part of No. 35 Beach Group, which would take part in the impending invasion of Italy. The Allies were gradually learning the techniques necessary to land and sustain an invading force on an enemy-held coast. In Brigadier Duncan's words, a beach group is 'a very complex formation whose sole object is to supply and feed an invading force, and to enable it to fight, until such time as it has been able to capture a port and get it working.... The work is highly technical and needs serious and strenous training for everyone'. After their initial training in Egypt, which included visits to the Syrian mountains, the group moved to Algeria for further training and their final preparations. During training, a Jodhpur team beat a Royal Army Ordnance Corps (RAOC) team – the professionals at this job – at identifying different ammunition types and their packs in darkness, much to the chagrin of the RAOC commanding officer.

They embarked in their landing craft and on the night of 8–9 September, landed on the Italian coast at Salerno. Although the Italian Army had surrendered, the German troops put up a vigorous defence. The assault troops went in at 3.30 a.m. and at 6.45 a.m. Majors Blakeman and Ram Singh landed on Red Beach, the latter becoming the first Indian soldier to set foot on mainland Europe. For the next seventeen days, until the port of Salerno was opened for use, the Jodhpurs were working at top pressure through the day and night, unloading and distributing stores. During this period, although the beach was shelled and machine-gunned, only one man had to be evacuated, deafened by an 88 mm shell bursting overhead, and there were eight others who were slightly wounded.

One company, under Captain Dungar Singh, was employed taking stores forward to the 5th Battalion the Sherwood Foresters, which was holding a position very close to the Germans in a particularly steep and difficult country. The only way they could be kept supplied with ammunition, water and food was by men on foot. On their way back down, the Jodhpurs always offered to carry any wounded men. The brigade commander wrote: 'All units under my command have spoken in the highest terms of the willing co-operation of all officers and men and of the hard work put in by them which enabled forward positions to be maintained where wheeled transport was unable to operate.'

For their service at Salerno, Major Ram Singh was awarded the DSO, Captain Dungar Singh the MC, and Jemadar Ganga Ram the MBE. Military medals were awarded to Quartermaster Havildar Bhoora Ram, Naik Shaitan Singh and Lance Naik Kishore Singh. In addition, seventeen officers and men from the unit were mentioned in despatches.

Their war was not over. After a spell as line-of-communication troops, the regiment in July 1944 received more up-to-date equipment, including anti-tank guns, and began battle-inoculation training. In December 1944 they joined the 10th Indian Brigade, 10th Indian Division, and the maharaja was able to visit them in camp at Forli in Italy. Later that month, there was a great deal of rain followed by heavy snowfall, and the four rifle companies were attached to experienced units in the front line. Training, particularly in patrolling, continued into January 1945. At the end of that month the regiment moved into the front line for the first time. They stayed there for a week before being relieved, and were back in the front line at the end of February, where they stayed until 22 March. By now the snow had thawed and deep mud made movement difficult. On 2 March the battalion became responsible for patrolling on the right and left battalion sectors of the Brigade front. Following a particularly successful platoon raid, the platoon commander, Jemadar Parbhu Singh, was awarded the MC.

On 8 April the regiment was transferred to the 25th Indian Infantry Brigade and occupied the Mount Caldaro position. This was a triangular position linked to the Monte Grande but German paratroops covered all three sides of the triangle, including the route along which all supplies had to pass. The battalion settled down to a programme of nightly patrols; the commanding officer of a neighbouring unit commented later that the regiment had earned a considerable reputation for the forcefulness of its patrolling. At the end of the month the battalion trained with the Churchill tanks of the 8th Royal Tank Regiment but this cooperation was never tested in battle as hostilities ended in Italy on 2 May 1945. The battalion embarked for India on 19 July, docked in Bombay on 29 July and arrived back in Jodhpur to a tumultuous reception on 2 August.

रण बंका राठौड़

Epilogue

AFTER INDEPENDENCE

In 1948, to celebrate the birth of the present Maharaja of Jodhpur, HH Gaj Singh II, a number of promotions and decorations were awarded to members of the State Forces. Majors Maharaj Prem Singh and Thakur Mohan Singh were both promoted to lieutenant colonel, and Lieutenant Colonel Kalyan Singh of the Jodhpur Lancers and Lieutenant Colonel Thakur Mohan Singh of the Durga Horse were awarded the State Awards of the Tazim, Gold and Hathi Saropao. The then maharaja, Hanwant Singh, made a point of dining in the Lancers' officers' mess at least once a week. It is said that the maharaja asked the commandant of the Jodhpur State Forces, Brigadier Zabar Singh (another grandson of Sir Pratap), whether Jodhpur could take on the Indian Army should Jodhpur wish to secede from the newly formed nation of India in a war of independence. The brigadier advised firmly against it but made it clear at the same time that he would do it if so ordered.

In 1948, General Chaudhari commanded the Indian Forces, which included the Jodhpur Lancers, in the Hyderabad Police Action. He asked one of his staff officers, Captain Kanwar Bijai Singh of the Jodhpur Lancers, what he would

Facing page: The royal arms of the Rathores carved into stone at the entrance of the Umaid Bhawan Palace, still the maharaja's official residence. The Lancers' motto, 'Ran Banka Rathore' (The Rathore – Invincible in Battle) is a proud part of the royal arms.

Risaldar Major and Honorary Captain (Retired) Umed Singh with his medals.

do if the Indian Army were to enter Jodhpur. 'In that case, Sir, I would go back to my regiment to face you!' The Jodhpur Lancers, loyal to their maharaja and to their state, could not be allowed to survive as well-trained and potent opponents to the Indian Army. Thus it was for a mixture of political and military reasons that the decision was taken, in 1951, to merge the State Forces into the Indian Army, with some units disappearing altogether. Although there was no longer a regimental polo team, the Jodhpur Lancers' soccer team won the Jodhpur District League in the last year of the regiment's existence, so maintaining their proud sporting tradition.

As far as the Jodhpur Lancers were concerned, some officers and men retired on pension. The remaining officers, together with some NCOs and sowars, were posted out to other units though the officers lost seniority on transfer. The largest group, six junior commissioned officers (JCOs) and some 250 NCOs and sowars, became 'D' Squadron of the 7th Light Cavalry with effect from August 1951. The 'D' Squadron was to be an experimental reconnaissance unit, mounted in armoured jeeps. The idea may have come from the exploits of the Special Air Service in the North African desert in the Second World War. The squadron was organized into three troops with fourteen jeeps each, together with mortar

The author with veterans in Jodhpur.

and anti-tank troops in support. A report dated 30 September 1951 states that selection for this new unit was done by the commanding officer of the 7th assisted by Major T.K. Theogras, the first squadron commander. The senior JCO was Risaldar Gyan Singh; the three troops were commanded by Risaldars Kishore Singh, Mukund Singh and Shambu Singh respectively; Risaldar Ridmal Singh commanded the anti-tank troop and Jemadar Umed Singh the mortar troop.

A report states that the men were 'very sincere and hard workers. Their spirits on the whole were high.' In 1952 the squadron took part in a two-sided tactical exercise, devised by Army HQ, on the Allahabad road, two miles from Kanpur. This exercise was observed by General Carriappa – at that time commander-in-chief of the Indian Army – together with other senior officers. At the end of the exercise, General Carriappa congratulated the men on their zest and zeal. The diligence and efficiency with which they carried out their task was much appreciated by the high-ranking observers. Collective training continued during the following four years and the unit took part in a number of other exercises at brigade and divisional levels. However, no decision was taken with regard

Amar Singh's medals.

to the future of what was, after all, an experimental unit. In 1956 they took part in an exercise in Jhansi and afterwards were inspected by Chief General Rajendra Singh, a Rajput related to the House of Jodhpur. The men complained to him about their unsatisfactory situation, being in limbo with no possibility of promotion, and he promised to look into the matter. In 1956 'D' Squadron, stationed at that time at Kapurthala in the Punjab, was divided into two and allocated partly to the 8th Cavalry and partly to the newly re-raised 20th Cavalry, who were equipped with the fast French AMX tanks armed with a 75 mm gun. Meanwhile the Durga Horse, which had been formed when the Lancers were mechanized and gave up their horses, had become part of the 61st Cavalry, a regiment which remains as the only mounted regiment in the modern Indian Army, apart from the President's Bodyguard.

So it was that the Jodhpur Lancers, like so many other famous regiments, faded into the mists of history. In its relatively short life of just over a hundred years, the regiment had fought in Europe, the Middle East and the Far East; from the muddy trenches of northern France to the bitter cold of a Chinese winter. Wherever the Jo Hokums went they gained an unrivalled reputation for excellence and efficiency, both on the battlefield and off it, resulting in a proud group of battle-honours and a long list of well-earned awards to individuals. Whatever they were asked to do, they did – and did it without complaint. Above all, that last great charge at Haifa represents a unique achievement in the history of warfare.

Lieutenant General Sir Henry (Harry) Chauvel (Australian Imperial Force) wrote in his despatches: 'The cavalry had to gallop over exposed ground against heavy rifle and machine gun fire, but it never faltered. Each wave of horsemen rode through the enemy, and those who were not killed threw up their hands.'

The thunder of hooves, the flashing swords and glittering lance-points may have gone forever but the eager listener can still hear the breeze carry a distant echo of that famous cry, 'Ran Banka Rathore!'

In January 2018, the beginning of the centenary year of Haifa, the Government of India changed the name of the Teen Murti statues roundabout in New Delhi to 'Haifa Chowk' in the presence of the prime ministers of both Israel and India.

Jodhpur Victory Medals; shoulder badge and cap badge.

Appendix 1

THE ORGANIZATION OF THE SARDAR RISALA IN 1889

When the regiment was founded, there were two regiments, each with 600 sowars, organized as follows:

Squadron officers	8
Risaldars	16
Jemadars	16
Kot Dafadars	16
Dafadars	96
Sowars	1058
Total	1210

All the recruits were inhabitants of Marwar, and were divided as follows:

Class	1st Regiment Squadron	2nd Regiment Squadron
Jodhas	1st	1st
Khichis	4th	4th
Mertias	2nd	3rd
Gogades	3rd	1st
Kaimkhanis	-	2nd

The horses were principally Arabs.

Pay rates were as follows:

Squadron officers	Rs 250 a month
Risaldars	Rs 80 to 125 a month
Jemadars	Rs 60 to 70 a month
Kot Dafadars	Rs 44 a month
Sowars	Rs 30 a month

Trumpeters and farriers were paid an extra Rs 5 a month. At this time a sowar in the regular cavalry would receive Rs 31 a month. A skilled Indian worker in civilian life would earn around Rs 12 a month but there would be deductions from a soldier's pay. During the Great War pay in the State Forces was brought up to par with that in the regular Indian Army. A rupee was one-fifteenth of a pound sterling during this period.

Appendix 2

THE COMMANDING OFFICERS OF THE SARDAR RISALA/JODHPUR LANCERS IN 1889-1947

Sir Pratap Singh	
Lt Col Hari (Hurjee) Singh	1900
Colonel Maharaj Sher Singhji	1914
Major Dalpat Singh MC	
Lt Col H.H. Holden	1918 (Killed in action)
Lt Col Pratap Singh	1908–1925
Lt Col Anop Singh	
Lt Col Jaswant Singh	
Lt Col Dalpat Singh	
Lt Col Thakur Prithi Singh	September 1936
Lt Col Thakur Bahadur Singh	September 1936–July 1941
Lt Col G.G. Collyns (3rd Cavalry)	July 1941–May 1942
Lt Col W.A.A. Loring (15th Lancers)	May 1942–March 1944
Lt Col R.G. Hanmer (6th Lancers)	March 1944–November 1944
Lt Col E.J.R. Emtage	November 1944–
Lt Col Kalyan Singh	
Lt Col Dhonkal Singh	
Lt Col Sultan Singh	

Appendix 3

THE OFFICERS OF THE JODHPUR LANCERS IN 1915

Major General Sir Pratap Singh, KCSI, GCVO, KCB: Honorary Colonel, the 34th Poona Horse

Major Sir Sarjan Singh, KCSI, Raja of Ratlam, Honorary Colonel, the 39th Central India Horse

Colonel-in-Chief: Maharaja Sumer Singh

Staff Officer to the Colonel-in-Chief: Thakur Dhonkal Singh

1st Lancers Sardar Risala; three squadrons of Rathore Rajputs and one squadron of Kaimkhanis

Commandant: Thakur Pratap Singh

Squadron Commanders:	Ram Singh Maharaj Akhai Singh Padam Singh Kishore Singh Kunwar Gaj Singh Thakur Dalpat Singh
Adjutant:	Mohbat Singh
Risaldar Major:	Panne Singh
Risaldars:	Hamid Khan Kesri Singh Himmat Singh Anop Singh Sabal Singh Kushal Singh Agar Singh

Jemadars:	Bhagwant Singh Agar Singh Kishan Singh Bahadur Singh Pem Singh Jethu Singh Dal Singh Chatersal Singh

---

Medical Officer: Prasono Kumar Ghose LMS, Assistant Surgeon
Veterinary Officer: Jemadar Khino Singh

By 1918 Squadron Commanders Ram Singh and Padam Singh, who joined the Army in 1879 and 1881 respectively, had left the regiment. Risaldar Major Panne Singh together with Risaldars Anop Singh and Kesrir Singh had all been promoted to command squadrons with the rank of captain. Bahadur Singh, Chatersal Singh and Pem Singh had been promoted to risaldar and there were a number of newly appointed jemadars, including Dool Singh IOM.
The 2nd Lancers Sardar Risala; four squadrons of Rathore Rajputs, temporarily reduced to three squadrons.

Commandant: Maharaj Sher Singh ADC

Squadron Commanders:	Kanwar Inder Singh Badan Singh Hira Lal Singh
Risaldar Major:	Aman Singh
Risaldars:	Jatan Singh Bhoor Singh Padam Singh Jiwan Singh Guman Singh

Jemadars	Bal Singh
	Bahadur Singh
	Hem Singh
	Mangal Singh
	Moti Singh
	Chator Singh
	Kolyan Singh

Medical Officer: Balwat R.R. Chandra Khandekar LMS
Veterinary Officer: Jemadar Madha Singh

By 1918, Kanwar Inder Singh was no longer with the regiment. He had been replaced by Captain Aman Singh Bahadur, the former risaldar major. Jatan Singh was now risaldar major.

The following British officers served with the regiment during the Great War:
Lieutenant Kunwar Daji Raj (27th Light Cavalry)
Major H.N. Holden (5th Cavalry)
Major A.D. Strong (10th Hodson's Horse)
Captain Mainyard (Veterinary Officer)
Captain E.L. Maxwell (11th Probyn's Horse)
Lt Col P.F. Gell (14th Lancers)
Major Ferguson (15th Lancers)
Lieutenant W. Chubb (36th Jacob's Horse)
Major A.J. Reynolds (37th Lancers)
Lieutenant A.B. Knight (4th Cavalry)
Captain H.F.P. Hornsby (5th Cavalry)
Lieutenant S. Clarke (34th Cavalry)
Captain C.E. Pert (37th Lancers)
Major A.B. Skinner (5th Cavalry)
Major G. Wheatly (27th Light Cavalry)
Major R.G.A. Trail (Guides Cavalry)

Appendix 4

THE OFFICERS OF THE JODHPUR LANCERS IN 1940

State Officers:	Lt Col Bahadur Singh*	Officer Commanding
	Major K. Shyam Singh	Second-in-Command
	Captain K. Arjun Singh	
	Captain K. Surajbhan Singh	
	Captain Kalyan Singh	
	Lieutenant K. Keshri Singh	Quartermaster
	Lieutenant Sultan Singh	Adjutant
	Lieutenant Chandan Singh	
	Lieutenant Thakur Jagat Singh	
	Lieutenant Dhonkal Singh	
	Lieutenant Bhopal Singh	
	Lieutenant K. Sardar Singh	
	Lieutenant K. Mohan Singh	
	2/Lt Ramdan Singh	
	2/Lt Prem Singh	
	2/Lt Mod Singh	
	2/Lt Kheem Singh	
Medical Officer:	2/Lt Tej Singh	
State Officer Cadets:	Pirthi Singh	
	Jabdi Khan	
British Officers:	Lt Col G.C. Collyns	3rd Cavalry
	Captain A.G.S. Alexander	Central India Horse
	Captain G.D.G. Garforth Bles	Guides Cavalry
Indian Officers:	Risaldar Major Chog Singh	
	Risaldar Amar Singh*	
	Risaldar Madan Singh*	

Risaldar Bhopal Singh
Risaldar Girdhari Singh
Jemadar Nathu Singh
Jemadar Sugan Singh
Jemadar Anop Singh
Jemadar Sadul Singh*
Jemadar Mangal Singh
Jemadar Madho Singh
Jemadar Bherun Singh
Jemadar Shambhu Singh
Jemadar Jai Singh
Jemadar Gulab Singh
Jemadar Amar Singh
Jemadar Jorawar Khan

---

*Served in the Great War

Appendix 5
THE ROLL OF HONOUR

Two sowars were killed in China in 1901 (see Chapter 2). These were Sowar Sheoram Singh and another whose name was unfortunately not recorded.

First World War

The Jodhpur Lancers served in France from the autumn of 1914 until the spring of 1918. The beautiful Indian Memorial at Neuve-Chapelle commemorates nearly 5,000 men of the Indian Army who laid down their lives in France during that period.

The memorial is circular in shape, with a 15-metre high column. It is guarded by two carved stone tigers, and is surmounted by a lotus capital and the Star of India. The following men of the Jodhpur Lancers are commemorated on this memorial:

Kot Dafadar	Baxe Singh	19.6.16
Kot Dafadar	Modh Singh	28.7.17
Dafadar	Dhool Singh	20.7.15 (Killed in action)
Dafadar	Hamir Singh	14.4.17
Dafadar	Khet Singh	20.12.14
Dafadar	Nahar Singh	20.7.15 (Killed in action)
L/Dafadar	Raghunath Singh	1.12.17 (Killed in action)
Sowar	Bagh Khan	24.12.14 (Killed in action)
Sowar	Bakhtawar Singh	22.3.16
Sowar	Bal Singh	22.7.16
Sowar	Banne Singh	9.5.17
Sowar	Bhairon Singh	1.12.17 (Killed in action)
Sowar	Bhawani Singh	13.3.17
Sowar	Bhopal Singh	13.9.17
Sowar	Bhun Singh	21.8.16
Sowar	Bijoi Singh	13.6.18

Sowar	Chand Singh	30.11.17
Sowar	Chatar Singh	3.2.17
Sowar	Dhankol Singh	20.2.18
Sowar	Dul Singh	21.1.15
Sowar	Gulab Singh	24.12.14 (Killed in action)
Sowar	Hamid Khan	1.12.17 (Killed in action)
Sowar	Hukam Singh	21.5.17
Sowar	Jatan Singh	20.10.17
Sowar	Jawand Singh	21.9.17
Sowar	Ladu Khan	4.12.17
Sowar	Lun Singh	23.5.17
Sowar	Magej Singh	20.8.16
Sowar	Magh Singh	21.12.16
Sowar	Makhan Singh	24.4.17
Sowar	Moti Singh	7.4.15
Sowar	Mul Singh 1053	16.11.17
Sowar	Mul Singh 1659	The CWGC have no information on this soldier
Sowar	Phul Singh	8.3.18
Sowar	Raghunath Singh	2.1.18
Sowar	Rewat Singh	11.4.16
Sowar	Sagat Singh	22.2.18
Sowar	Samdar Singh	20.7.15 (Killed in action)
Sowar	Sardar Singh	20.12.14 (Killed in action)
Sowar	Sohan Singh	1.12.17 (Killed in action)
Follower	Himativa	10.2.17

The names of the following Alwar Lancers, who served with the Jodhpur Lancers, are recorded on the same memorial:

L/Dafadar	Raghunath Singh
Sowar	Bhanwar Singh
Sowar	Makhan Singh
Sowar	Mul Singh

The following names are commemorated in the Meerut Military Cemetery, St Martin, Boulogne:

Captain	Thakur Ragunath Singh (ADC to the Raja of Ratlam)	15.6.15
L/Dafadar	Jawal Singh	17.3.15
Sowar	Chatar Singh	2.2.15
Sowar	Deo Singh	18.3.15
Sowar	Hari Singh	4.4.15
Sowar	Khim Singh	22.12.14
Sowar	Mul Singh	26.4.15
Follower	Bhooria	21.2.15
Follower	Chhailio	2.2.15
Follower	Ganglio	26.3.15

With the exception of Sowar Khim Singh, who died of wounds, the remainder of these men all died of pneumonia or bronchitis.

The following were commemorated at a memorial in the Marzagues Military Cemetery, Marseilles:

L/Dafadar	Ful Singh	20.7.17
Sowar	Bhopal Singh	13.12.17
Sowar	Bhur Singh	20.6.17
Sowar	Dal Singh	28.7.16
Sowar	Dul Singh	2.2.18
Sowar	Lal Singh	10.12.16
Sowar	Mul Singh	2.10.17
Sowar	Nathu Khan	24.5.17
Sowar	Sardar	9.10.17
Sowar	Sheonath Singh	27.11.16
Follower	Tejia	24.10.16

Captain R.G.A. Trail of the QVO Corps of Guides Cavalry was attached briefly to the Jodhpur Lancers. He was killed at Villers Guislan on 1 December 1917 and is buried in Tincourt Cemetery nearby. Lt Kanwar Daji Raj of the Indian Land Forces was also killed while attached to the regiment, on 23 September 1917.

Headstones of other members of the regiment are to be found in France:

Sowar Jitu Khan	St Sever Cemetery, Rouen	30.3.17
Sowar Kehar Singh	Neuville-sous-Montreuil Indian Cemetery Died of enteric fever	16.2.15
Follower Shivram	St Riquier Military Cemetery, Somme Died of pneumonia	28.12.16

Wounded in France:

Colonel	Maharaj Sher Singh	14.9.15
Risaldar	Hem Singh	17.8.16
Risaldar	Pem Singh	30.11.17
Jemadar	Ker Singh	6.8.16
Kot Dafadar	Badan Singh	19.4.15
Dafadar	Dhan Singh	15.9.15
Dafadar	Din Singh	21.7.16
Dafadar	Durjan Singh	1.12.17
Dafadar	Khuman Singh	15.9.15
Dafadar	Roop Singh	6.8.16
L/Dafadar	Bulidan Singh	18.8.17
L/Dafadar	Jawar Singh 661	22.7.16
L/Dafadar	Jawar Singh 1004	14.2.15
L/Dafadar	Jog Singh	31.8.16
L/Dafadar	Khaju Singh	1.12.17
L/Dafadar	Partap Singh	20.12.14
L/Dafadar	Phool Singh	20.12.14
L/Dafadar	Sardar Singh	1.12.17
L/Dafadar	Samel Singh	9.2.15
Sowar	Achal Singh	9.4.17
Sowar	Azim Khan	1.12.17

Sowar	Bahadur Singh	12.11.17
Sowar	Bakhtawar Singh	1.12.17
Sowar	Bhaboot Singh	22.7.16
Sowar	Chater Singh	1.12.17
Sowar	Dhoor Singh	15.8.16
Sowar	Ganpat Singh	17.8.16
Sowar	Gulab Khan	16.9.16
Sowar	Harnath Singh 1671	16.9.16
Sowar	Harnath Singh 2255	1.12.17
Sowar	Jabdi Khan	16.9.16
Sowar	Janak Singh	12.11.17
Sowar	Junjar singh	6.8.16
Sowar	Jaswant Singh	4.12.17
Sowar	Jawan Singh	9.2.15
Sowar	Khum Singh	2.12.17
Sowar	Kishen Singh	2.12.17
Sowar	Mool Singh	21.7.16
Sowar	Nandhu Singh	30.10.16
Sowar	Onar Singh	12.12.17
Sowar	Peet Singh	20.12.14
Sowar	Ram Singh	6.8.16
Sowar	Ranjit Singh 1164	6.8.16
Sowar	Ranjit Singh 1274	1.12.17
Sowar	Sagar Singh	11.4.17
Sowar	Sheolal Singh	14.9.15
Sowar	Shivdan Singh	16.5.17
Sowar	Shivji Singh	1.12.17
Sowar	Takhat Singh	9.2.15
Sowar	Udai Singh	11.4.17
Sowar	Ugam Singh	17.5.17
Sowar	Umar Khan	3.12.17
Cook	Sheojo	14.9.15
Servant	Tar Singh	14.9.15
Sweeper	Sheo Karnia	14.9.15

The Jodhpur Lancers served in Palestine in 1918, where the following seventeen members of the regiment were killed in action:

Lt Col	Hyla Holden (5th Cavalry)	26.10.18	Aleppo
Jemadar	Assu Singh IOM	14.7.18	Jordan Valley
Jemadar	Khang Singh IOM	14.7.18	Jordan Valley
Dafadar	Man Singh	14.7.18	Jordan Valley
Dafadar	Koom Singh	14.7.18	Jordan Valley
L/Dafadar	Rewat Singh	14.7.18	Jordan Valley
L/Dafadar	Khet Singh	14.7.18	Jordan Valley
Sowar	Azam Khan	14.7.18	Jordan Valley
Sowar	Hussain Khan	14.7.18	Jordan Valley
Sowar	Bhoor Singh	14.7.18	Jordan Valley
Sowar	Khandoo Singh	14.7.18	Jordan Valley
Sowar	Aman Singh	14.7.18	Jordan Valley
Sowar	Paney Singh	14.7.18	Jordan Valley
Sowar	Baloo Singh	14.7.18	Jordan Valley
Sowar	Tagat Singh	23.9.18	Haifa
Sowar	Shazad Singh	23.9.18	Haifa
Sowar	Junjar Singh	26.10.18	Aleppo

Died of wounds received in action:

Major	Thakur Dalpat Singh	23.9.18	Haifa
Trumpet Major	Sher Singh IOM Died 15.11	23.9.18	Haifa
Dafadar	Dhombal Singh Died 27.9	23.9.18	Haifa
Sowar	Gopal Singh Died 30.9	23.9.18	Haifa
Sowar	Sultan Singh Died 18.10	23.9.18	Haifa

Missing:

L/Dafadar	Bher Singh	14.7.18	Jordan Valley
Sowar	Ladhoo Khan	14.7.18	Jordan Valley
Sowar	Musharaf Khan	14.7.18	Jordan Valley
Sowar	Kan Singh	14.7.18	Jordan Valley
Sowar	Dool Singh	14.7.18	Jordan Valley

Taken prisoner but later released:

Dafadar	Samel Singh	14.7.18	Jordan Valley
Sowar	Bacham Singh	14.7.18	Jordan Valley

Wounded:

Captain	Henry Fyshe-Palmer Hornsby MC (5th Cavalry)	26.10.18	Aleppo
Jemadar	Jawan Singh IDSM	14.7.18	Jordan Valley
Jemadar	Pith Singh 1137	23.9.18	Haifa
Jemadar	Gardham Singh	23.9.18	Haifa
Jemadar	Berisal Singh	23.9.18	Haifa
Jemadar	Pith Singh 1089	26.10.18	Aleppo
Jemadar	Bahadur Singh IDSM	26.10.18	Aleppo
Kot Dafadar	Mahdo Singh	23.9.18	Haifa
Dafadar	Gomand Singh	14.7.18	Jordan Valley
Dafadar	Amar Singh IOM	14.7.18	Jordan Valley
Dafadar	Ram Singh	23.9.18	Haifa
Dafadar	Bhorn Singh (Alwar Lancers)	26.10.18	Aleppo
L/Dafadar	Daul Singh	14.7.18	Jordan Valley
L/Dafadar	Ranjit Singh	23.9.18	Haifa
Sowar	Isla Khan	14.7.18	Jordan Valley
Sowar	Mool Singh	14.7.18	Jordan Valley

Sowar	Deo Singh	14.7.18	Jordan Valley
Sowar	Dhoor Singh	23.9.18	Haifa
Farrier	Panmai Singh	23.9.18	Haifa
Farrier	Fateh Singh	23.9.18	Haifa
Sowar	Beli Singh	23.9.18	Haifa
Sowar	Garia Singh	23.9.18	Haifa
Sowar	Chati Singh	23.9.18	Haifa
Sowar	Lall Singh	23.9.18	Haifa
Sowar	Nag Singh	23.9.18	Haifa
Trumpeter	Arjan Singh	26.10.18	Aleppo
Sowar	Mod Singh	26.10.18	Aleppo
Sowar	Bachan Singh	26.10.18	Aleppo
Sowar	Mandoo Khan	26.10.18	Aleppo
Sowar	Phool Singh (Alwar Lancers)	26.10.18	Aleppo
Farrier	Man Singh	26.10.18	Aleppo

Second World War

Killed in an accident: Major K. Surajbhan Singh
Died of Tuberculosis: Major Sujan Singh
Killed in a road-traffic accident: Daf/Major Kalyan Singh

Appendix 6
HONOURS AND AWARDS

Battle Honours

Hazara 1891
NWF of India 1897–98
China 1900
Cambrai 1917
France and Flanders 1914–18
Megiddo
Sharon
Damascus
Palestine 1918

Decorations

The highest-ranking award specific to the Indian Empire was the Most Exalted Order of the Star of India, established in 1861 and restricted to the very highest ranks. The Order of British India (OBI) was instituted in 1837 and consisted of two classes. The First Class, restricted to risaldars (subedars in the infantry) and above, carried with it the title 'Sardar Bahadur' – literally 'The Brave One' or 'Chief'. The Second Class, open to jemadars, carried the title 'Bahadur'. Both awards brought with them a small increase in pay. The Indian Order of Merit (IOM), also instituted in 1837 and consisting of three classes, was open to any Indian officer or soldier, regardless of rank, and was awarded for an act of conspicuous gallantry in the face of the enemy. This is the oldest award for gallantry in the British Empire, pre-dating the Victoria Cross. A man's first act of bravery gave him admission to the Third Class, a second act by the same man gave him admission to the Second Class and, extremely rarely, a third act of bravery gained him the First Class award. All three classes included an increase in pay. In 1911, Indian officers and other ranks became eligible for the award of the Victoria Cross (VC) and accordingly the First Class IOM was abolished. In 1917, Indian officers became eligible for the Military Cross (MC).

The Indian Distinguished Service Medal (IDSM) was introduced in 1907 as an award to recognize distinguished service by officers, non-commissioned officers and men of the Indian land forces. The Indian Meritorious Service Medal (IMSM) was established in 1888 and was granted, with a small annuity, to soldiers with eighteen or more years of meritorious service. However, very few were awarded before 1914. In addition to all of the above awards, Indian soldiers were entitled to the appropriate campaign medals.

Sir Pratap Singh, promoted to lieutenant general in the British Army, 3 June 1916. Knight Commander of the Star of India (1886), Grand Cross of the Star of India (1897), Grand Cross of the Royal Victorian Order (1911), Grand Cross of the Order of the Bath (Military) (1901), Legion d'Honneur, Order of the Nile (1st Class) Hon LLD (Cantab).

China 1900–01

Dafadar Dool Singh	IOM, 3rd Class

France 1914–17

Commandant	Thakur Partap Singh (Sardar Bahadur)	OBI, 1st Class
Squadron Commander	Aman Singh, Bahadur	OBI, 2nd Class
Squadron Commander	Anop Singh, Bahadur	OBI, 2nd Class, Croix de Guerre
Captain (Squadron Commander)	Paney Singh, Bahadur	OBI, 2nd Class
Risaldar	Agar Singh, Bahadur	OBI, 2nd Class
Sowar	Moti Singh	IOM, 2nd Class
Sowar	Gulab Singh	IOM, 2nd Class
Sowar	Dhoukal Singh	IOM, 2nd Class
Dafadar	Aidan Singh	IDSM
Dafadar	Bhoor Singh	IDSM
Dafadar	Bhur Singh	IDSM
Dafadar	Chander Singh	IDSM

Dafadar	Chiman Singh	IDSM
Dafadar	Roop Singh	IDSM (Later Lieutenant)
L/Dafadar	Zallim Singh	IDSM
Sowar	Bahadur Singh	IDSM
Sowar	Man Singh	IDSM
Sowar	Mool Singh	IDSM
Dafadar	Arjun Singh	IMSM
Dafadar	Balwant Singh	IMSM
Dafadar	Jog Singh	IMSM
Dafadar	Samel Singh	IMSM
Dafadar	Surajbux Singh	IMSM
Sowar	Ashraf Khan	IMSM
Sowar	Jog Singh	IMSM
Sowar	Mool Singh	IMSM
Sowar	Sultan Singh	IMSM
Farrier	Khoom Singh	IMSM

Palestine 1918

Lt Col	H.N. Holden	DSO Mention in Despatches
Major	P.F. Gell	DSO Mention in Despatches
Major	A.J. Reynolds	DSO
Major	Thakur Dalpat Singh	MC
Captain	Thakur Anop Singh	MC IOM (2nd Class)
Captain	H.F.P. Hornsby	MC
Captain	Aman Singh Bahadur	IOM (2nd Class)
Captain	Khim Singh	Mention in Despatches
Captain	Sankar Narain Singh	Mention in Despatches
Lieutenant	A.B. Knight	MC
2/Lt	Kanwar Sagat Singh	MC
Risaldar	Shaitan Singh Bahadur	IOM (2nd Class)
Risaldar	Keshen Singh Bahadur	IOM (2nd Class)
Jemadar	Asoo Singh Bahadur	IOM (2nd Class)
Jemadar	Khang Singh Bahadur	IOM (2nd Class)

Dafadar	Amar Singh	IOM (2nd Class)
Lieutenant	Bahadur Singh	IDSM (later Captain)
Risaldar	Jog Singh	IDSM
Jemadar	Jawar Singh	IDSM
Jemadar	Bishen Singh	IDSM
Jemadar	Bahadur Singh	IDSM
Trumpet Major	Sher Singh	IOM (2nd Class)
Dafadar	Khajn Singh	Mention in Despatches
Dafadar	Amer Singh	IOM (2nd Class)
Dafadar	Jor Singh	IOM (2nd Class)
Dafadar	Doong Singh	IDSM
Dafadar	Jog Singh	IDSM
Dafadar	Mohabat Singh	IDSM
Dafadar	Moti Singh	IDSM
L/Dafadar	Aidem Singh	IDSM
L/Dafadar	Bijai Singh	IDSM
L/Dafadar	Bharon Singh	IDSM
L/Dafadar	Banwan Singh	IDSM
L/Dafadar	Dhonkal Singh	IDSM
L/Dafadar	Khang Singh	IDSM
Sowar	Amar Singh	IDSM
Sowar	Bagh Singh	IDSM
Sowar	Bahadur Singh	IDSM
Sowar	Bhim Singh	IDSM
Sowar	Bhoor Singh	IDSM
Sowar	Bishen Singh	IDSM
Sowar	Guman Singh	IDSM
Sowar	Gunpat Singh	IDSM
Sowar	Padam Singh	IDSM
Sowar	Jagat Singh	IDSM
Sowar	Kesri Singh	IDSM
Sowar	Sanwat Singh	IDSM
Daf/Major	Suraj Baksh Singh	IMSM (Later Jemadar)
Kot Dafadar	Bishen Singh	IMSM

Kot Dafadar	Berisal Singh	IMSM
Kot Dafadar	Kan Singh	IMSM
Kot Dafadar	Pithi Singh	IMSM
Dafadar	Bakhtawar Singh	IMSM
Dafadar	Baney Singh	IMSM
Dafadar	Bishan Singh	IMSM
Dafadar	Doong Singh	IMSM
Dafadar	Brisal Singh	IMSM
Dafadar	Gain Singh	IMSM
Dafadar	Gigai Singh	IMSM
Dafadar	Jog Singh	IMSM
Dafadar	Kalyan Singh	IMSM
Dafadar	Khanu Singh	IMSM
Dafadar	Mod Singh	IMSM
Dafadar	Udai Singh	IMSM
L/Dafadar	Dhoka Singh	IMSM
L/Dafadar	Gobind Singh	IMSM
L/Dafadar	Khang Singh	IMSM
L/Dafadar	Sultan Singh	IMSM
Sowar	Bakhtawar Singh	IMSM
Sowar	Baksho Singh Khan	IMSM
Sowar	Birad Singh	IMSM
Sowar	Dan Singh	IMSM
Sowar	Gain Singh	IMSM
Sowar	Gobul Singh	IMSM
Sowar	Jawan Singh	IMSM
Sowar	Kalu Singh	IMSM
Sowar	Khang Singh	IMSM
Sowar	Meg Singh	IMSM
Sowar	Mug Singh	IMSM
Sowar	Mool Singh	IMSM
Sowar	Paduban Singh	IMSM
Sowar	Pithi Singh	IMSM
Sowar	Rawat Singh	IMSM

Sowar	Rud Singh	IMSM
Sowar	Tej Singh	IMSM
Farrier	Jagat Singh	IMSM
Farrier	Mukan Singh	IMSM

In India

Major	Kishore Singh	OBI
Dafadar	Bage Khan	IMSM
Dafadar	Magan Singh	IMSM
L/Dafadar	Deo Singh	IMSM

Between the Wars

Lt Col	Thakur Anop Singh MC, IOM,	OBI 1st Class
Lt Col	Bahadur Singh	OBI 2nd Class
Major (Hon. Lt Col)	Hem Singh	OBI 2nd Class
Risaldar	Udai Singh	OBI, 2nd class
Dafadar	Jor Singh	IDSM
Kot Dafadar	Kan Singh	IMSM
Dafadar	Bakhtawar Singh	IMSM
Dafadar	Doong Singh	IMSM
Dafadar	Daulat Khan	IMSM
Dafadar	Kalyan Singh	IMSM
Dafadar	Kannu Singh	IMSM
Dafadar	Udai Singh	IMSM
L/Dafadar	Jawar Singh	IMSM
Sowar	Bakshu Singh	IMSM
Sowar	Brid Singh	IMSM
Sowar	Gokul Singh	IMSM
Sowar	Kalu Singh	IMSM
Sowar	Magh Singh	IMSM
Sowar	Taj Singh	IMSM
Sowar	Rug Singh	IMSM

Second World War

Captain Girdhari Singh	Quartermaster	MBE	January 1946
Lt Col E.J.R Emtage	Mention in Despatches	Gallant and distinguished service in Italy	

Unfortunately, no complete list of those members of the regiment who were entitled to campaign and other medals appears to have survived. The State Forces List for 1919 gives the names and ranks of the following officers – then serving with the regiment – as entitled to medals:

Punjab Frontier 1897–98, with the clasp 'Tirah'

Resaldar Pem Singh. He also held the Queen's South Africa Medal 1890–1902 with clasps for 'Transvaal', 'Paardeburg', and 'Cape Colony', presumably awarded for service with another regiment, since the Jodhpur Lancers did not serve in South Africa.
Risaldar Khuman Singh.
Risaldar Shetan Singh. Also held the Queen's South Africa Medal 1890–1902 with clasps for 'Transvaal', 'Paardeburg', and 'Cape Colony' and the King's South Africa Medal.
Jemadar Badan Singh. He also held the Queen's South Africa Medal 1890–1902 with the clasp 'Cape Colony' and the King's South Africa Medal.

The China Medal

Commandant Pratap Singh Bahadur
Squadron Commander Maharaj Akhol Singh
Squadron Commander Panne Singh
Squadron Commander Kesri Singh
Squadron Commander Anop Singh
Squadron Commander Bahadur Singh
Risaldar Major Sabal Singh

Risaldar Khuman Singh, who also held the Punjab Frontier Medal with the clasp for 'Tirah'
Risaldar Kushal Singh
Risaldar Padam Singh
Jemadar Dool Singh IOM
Jemadar Khiv Singh
Assistant Surgeon Prosano Kumar Ghose, who also held the medal for the Punjab Frontier 1897–98

London Coronation Medal

Commandant Thakur Pratab Singh
Squadron Commander Panne Singh
Jemadar Dool Singh IOM

Delhi Durbar Medal

Commandant Thakur Pratab Singh
Squadron Commander Kesri Singh
Jemadar Sajjan Singh
Secretary Shanker Lal BA

A memorial was erected on the site of the action at Haritan, north-west of Aleppo. This marks the site of the last action fought in the Middle East, with a list of units engaged and a roll of honour of those killed or who died of wounds. It is not known whether this memorial survives. It was proposed that a general memorial on the west bank of the Suez Canal near Katara be erected to commemorate the services of the 15th Imperial Service Brigade, although it is not known whether this was ever done. The Teen Murti memorial in Delhi, which commemorates the services of the Brigade, may have been erected instead.

Appendix 7
THE UNIFORMS OF THE JODHPUR LANCERS

As far as can be ascertained, no examples of a sowar's full dress, pre-1914 uniform survives, though there is what appears to be an officer's kurta in the Indian Army Museum in the Red Fort, Delhi. The sword and waist belts certainly appear identical to those worn by Sir Pratap Singh in photographs. For details of the sowar's uniforms we are therefore forced to rely on illustrations. Fortunately Major A.C. Lovett produced at least two watercolours showing the men of the regiment; the originals of these are now in the National Army Museum, London. The first, entitled *Jodhpur Sardar Risala*, is signed and dated 1910 and is reproduced in *The Armies of India* by Lieutenant General Sir George MacMunn. The second watercolour, of a dismounted dafadar, is neither signed nor dated but would appear to be of around the same period. Both men wear plain white kurtas and breeches with dark blue puttees and black boots. Both wear a brass *cheel* (kite) on the upper right arm; the dafadar's badge is on a red cloth backing, as are his gold rank stripes, but the sowar does not appear to have a cloth backing to his badge. The colour of the cummerbunds is best described as 'light red' – a brownish shade – or possibly 'Venetian red', which is a little brighter. Certainly, neither of these is bright red or scarlet and one must assume that this is deliberate. Brown leather belts are worn. The upper half of the sowar's lance pennon is the same colour as the cummerbund, the lower half being white. The turbans are mid-grey-blue, with bands of white. The sowar has stripes of the same colour as his cummerbund in the white bands while the stripes in the dafadar's white bands are dark blue or black. Both men wear white tufts, out of which rise the typical Rajput tinsel aigrette (hooked plume) – silver for the sowar and gold for the dafadar. The dafadar's sword has a plain steel hilt with no guard and a light-brown leather sword knot and scabbard of the same colour with a brass tip. The sowar's scabbard is black with a brass tip and his horse's harness and saddle are dark brown. Though the *State Forces Army Lists* states that the 1st risala had dark grey facings, with dark green for the 2nd risala, both with orange lance pennons, no evidence has been found to substantiate this statement.

In the absence of any photographic evidence, one can only assume that the troops in France wore khaki uniforms similar to the ones worn by other Indian troops, with regimental shoulder titles. *The Indian Army 1914–1947,* produced by Osprey Publishing, carries a picture of a dismounted dafadar in Palestine in 1918. Unfortunately, no source is quoted for this illustration. The Mysore Lancer in the background is taken from a watercolour by A.E. Haswell Miller, dated 1922, but this group of Indian soldiers does not include a Jodhpur Lancer. The dafadar wears a light khaki kurta and breeches, with brown leather belts, gaiters and boots. The scabbard is also brown leather with a brass tip; the sword has a plain steel hilt without a guard and a brown leather sword knot. The dafadar's turban is a plain, very light green/khaki and his cummerbund is pale pink without the brownish tinge of the Lovett illustrations. His brass *cheel* is surmounted by two crossed lances, all on a red cloth background (a kot dafadar?). On his cloth epaulette is the brass title 'Jodhpur' over 'Lancers', the lettering being set in two arcs so as to produce the overall effect of a pointed ellipse. (There is an example of this type of shoulder title in the Imperial War Museum, Lambeth.) The corresponding badge for the infantry has the lettering in two straight lines. The dafadar's rank stripes are white on a khaki backing and he has four blue service stripes and one red wound stripe on his lower right arm. He has two medal ribbons but it is not clear what these are intended to represent.

The situation with regard to officer's uniforms is somewhat easier as we have a number of portraits and photographs to draw upon. Richard Simkin, in his series of plates titled *Types of the Indian Army*, includes a portrait of Sir Pratap, which is almost certainly based on the excellent photograph taken when the latter visited England in 1897 for the jubilee. The folds of Sir Pratap's turban are white on the left side and gold on the right, with white bars edged dark blue. There is a red tuft just to the left of centre, from which emerges a gold and silver aigrette and a dark-blue brooch bearing a portrait of Queen Victoria; the brooch edged with pearls around the portrait of the queen was worn on the right side of the turban. His kurta is white with lavish gold lace on the collar, upper arms, cuffs and hem. Gloves are not worn. Shoulder cords and aiguillette are gold, and around his neck is the ribbon – blue edged with white – of the Order of British India; he has the Jubilee Medal and a gold star on his left breast. His sword and waist belts are white with gold edges and the waist belt buckle is gold with a silver

Officers of the Jodhpur Lancers.

monogram. The red cummerbund is heavily ornamented in gold. Breeches are plain white and he wears high black cavalry boots. His scabbard is black leather with a steel tip. The sword appears to have a Mameluke-style hilt, possibly ivory-mounted. His saddle and harness are brown leather decorated in gilt, with a red throat plume. A group photograph taken in 1897 includes Sir Pratap, Major Turner of the Viceroy's Bodyguard and a young officer of the Jodhpur Lancers who may well be Thakur Hari Singh. This officer is wearing the India General Service Medal with a bar, presumably for the Tirah campaign. The lace on his cuffs is of a different design to that of Sir Pratap and his turban is folded rather differently, with the plain white to his right and the gold on the left.

This illustration has similarities with later portraits. Kurtas are always white and lavishly ornamented with gold lace on the collar, upper arms, cuffs and half-way down the chest. Sometimes the hem is also trimmed with gold lace. There may be a white 'light' showing on the collar, depending upon the width of the lace. Waist and sword belts are white leather overlaid with gold lace so as to leave a central white stripe. The waist buckle is silver, with a monogram in the earlier cases, and other fittings are gold as are the shoulder cords. The monogram is not easy to untangle but appears to consist of three letters – R, S and C – in silver, surrounded by a silver wreath on a hammered gilt background. The 'R' and 'S' might stand for Sardar Risala, in which case might one expect a 'J' for Jodhpur? Cummerbunds are red, heavily embroidered with gold. Turbans vary but light blue and gold appear as a common combination with gold ornaments. Black leather Wellington boots are worn. Scabbards are steel with gilt sword hilts. A photograph of Stuart Beatson shows him wearing the Indian Mutiny Medal 1857, the Afghanistan Medal 1878–80, the Egypt Medal 1882–89 and the Khedive's Star 1882–91. Officers in France, during the First World War, wear the standard British khaki service dress, though Sir Pratap wears a longer jacket of his own design.

An interesting colour photograph, currently in the Risala dining room at the Umaid Bhawan Palace, shows Sir Pratap, Maharaja Sardar Singh and Colonel Beatson together, and so was presumably taken sometime during the five years while the colonel was in Jodhpur. Sir Pratap wears the Jodhpur Lancers' uniform as described above, with the sash of the Order of British India. However, the maharaja and the colonel are both wearing British Hussar Officers' uniforms, the latter with a red and gold turban! The maharaja wears the distinctive pouch belt of the 10th Hussars while the colonel's red collar suggests the 3rd Hussars. Note that their sabretaches bear the distinctive *cheel* in silver. It is not at all clear, though, why they should be wearing these uniforms. Colonel Beatson does not appear to have served in the Hussars, nor is there any record in the regimental history of the 10th Hussars of any link between Jodhpur and the 10th. The regiment was serving in India at this time and they did escort the Prince of Wales, who was colonel of the regiment, on a tour of Scinde. Is this when the young maharaja was given permission to wear the uniform of the Prince of Wales' own regiment? All three men are wearing the aiguillettes of a staff appointment so perhaps they were temporarily attached to the staff of the Prince of Wales. In this picture the maharaja wears a blue side-cap piped gold but it is not possible to make out the badge. In another portait he wears the same uniform with a red and gold turban, though folded differently than Colonel Beatson's.

Full dress seems finally to have given way to khaki in the mid-thirties. The cap badge during the First World War was a *cheel* facing left on two crossed lances with the title 'Jodhpur' over 'Lancers' (see *Military Badges of the British Empire 1914–18* by R.H.W. Cox, published in 1983 by the Standard Art Book Co. of Chicago). By the Second World War the lances seem to have been dropped from the cap badge. Cloth shoulder titles of a warm pink, with dark-blue lettering were worn. Black and white photographs, probably taken at the training centre, show armoured cars marked with a dark (probably black) square on the lower left mudguard with letters in (perhaps) white JL over a number (the photographs are not very clear, hence the lack of clarity). Whether other unit insignia was used is not known.

NOTES

Introduction

1 Amar Singh's diary provides a fascinating account of the daily life of an Indian living on the boundary between two societies – British and Indian – through a period of great change. The interested reader is referred to *Reversing the Gaze* by Sussanne Rudolph, Lloyd Rudolph and Mohan Singh Kanota (New Delhi, Oxford University Press, 2000) and *Between Two Worlds* by DeWitt C. Ellinwood (Lanham, Maryland, Hamilton Books, 2005).

2 This quotation is taken from *The House of Marwar* by Dhananajaya Singh, New Delhi, Roli Books, 1994.

3 This quotation is taken from *India Companion* by Louis Nicholson, London, Headline Book Publishing, 1996.

4 This quotation is taken from *The House of Marwar* by Dhananajaya Singh.

5 This quotation, and the three which follow, are all taken from *The House of Marwar* by Dhananajaya Singh.

6 This quotation is taken from a record of the speech in the Royal Archives at Windsor and reproduced by gracious permission of Her Majesty the Queen.

7 *A Matter of Honour* by Philip Mason, London, Jonathan Cape, 1974.

Chapter 1: The Early Years

1 This quotation is taken from *The House of Marwar* by Dhananajaya Singh.

2 The term 'sardar' denotes nobility. It also means 'chief', and the fact that clan chiefs were encouraged to enlist or, at the very least, to send their eldest son to join the new regiment, may have led to the unit's title. 'Risala' simply means cavalry.

Chapter 3: France 1914–18

1 These excerpts, and others later in the work, are from a selection of extracts from the letters to and from Indian soldiers serving in France, which were used for a monthly summary on the troops morale prepared by the chief censor. They may be found in the India and Oriental Collection of the British Library L/MIL/5/825, 826 and 827. A selection has been published in *Indian Voices of the Great War* by David Omissi, London, Macmillan Press Ltd, 1999.

BIBLIOGRAPHY

Allen, C., and Sharada Dwivedi (1988). *Lives of the Indian Princes.* Mumbai, eESHWAR, an imprint of Business Publications Inc.

Amar Singh's Diary: the original manuscript is now in the care of his great nephews, Man Singh and Prithvi Singh of Kanota.

Anglesey, the Marquis of (1994). *A History of British Cavalry*, Volume 5: 1914–19, Egypt, Palestine & Syria. *London, Leo Cooper.*

Annual Review of the Working of the Indian State Forces – various years. India Office Library, L/MIL/17/6/67–71.

Anonymous (1945). *Jodhpur's Contribution to Victory*. Jodhpur Government Press.

Beatson, Brigadier General S. (1903). *Imperial Service Troops of the Native States: A History.* Calcutta, Office of the Superintendent of Government Printing, India.

Bhatia, H.S., ed. (1977). *Military History of British India (1607–1947).* New Delhi, Deep and Deep Publications.

Duncan, Major General R.C. (1946). *The History of the Jodhpur State Forces in the War 1939–45.* Jodhpur, Jodhpur Government Press.

Falls, Captain C. and Major A.F. Becke (1930). *Military Operations in Egypt and Palestine from June 1917 until the end of the War*, Part II Volume 2. HMSO.

Gaylor, J. (1992). *Sons of John Company: The Indian and Pakistan Armies 1903–1991.* Tunbridge Wells, Spellmount Publishers Ltd.

Harfield, A. (1990). *The Indian Army of the Empress 1861–1903.* Tunbridge Wells, Spellmount Publishers Ltd.

Harrington, P. (2001). *Peking 1900: The Boxer Rebellion.* Oxford, Osprey Publishing.

Head, R., and T. McClenaghan (1998). *The Armies of the Indian Princely States: Volume 1: An Historical Overview.* Milton Keynes, the Military Press.

Heathcote, T.A. (1974). *The Indian Army: The Garrison of British Imperial India 1822–1922.* Newton Abbot, David and Charles.

Hervey, Major C. (1968). 'Gallop to Aleppo', *Journal of the United Services Institute*, Number 113, p. 155 et seq.

HMSO (1920). *History of the 15th (IS) Cavalry Brigade during the Great War 1914–18.* London.

Indian State Forces Annual Reports – various years. India Office Library, L/MIL/17/6/56 et seq.

Indian State Forces Lists – various years. India Office Library, L/MIL/17/6/51 et seq.

Ismay, General Lord (1960). *Memoirs of Lord Ismay.* London, Heinemann.

J.B. Hayward and Sons (1931). *Honours and Awards to the Indian Army, August 1914 to August 1921.* London.

Jodhpur State Forces List 1939. Jodhpur Government Press.

Jodhpur's Contribution to Victory (1945). Jodhpur Government Press.

Keay, J. (2000). *India: A History.* London, HarperCollins.

Kempton, C. (2003). *Loyalty and Honour: The Indian Army 1939–1947 Part 1: Divisions.* Milton Keynes, the Military Press.

Mason, P. (1974). *A Matter of Honour: An Account of the Indian Army, its Officers and Men.* London, Jonathan Cape.

Maunsell, Colonel E.B. (1926). *Prince of Wales's Own: The Scinde Horse: 1839–1922.* Published privately.

Maxwell, Captain E.L. (1914). *A History of XI King Edward's Own Lancers (Probyn's Horse)*. Guilford, A.C. Curtis Ltd.

Maxwell, Lieutenant Colonel E.L. (1890–1916). Letters of Lt Colonel Eustace Maxwell. Unpublished. National Army Museum 7402-34.

Nicholson, L. (1996). *India Companion* London, Headline Book Publishing.

Norie, E.W.M. (1903). *Official Account of the Military Operations in China 1900–01.* London, HMSO.

Perrett, B. (1999). *Megiddo 1918: The Last Great Cavalry Victory.* Oxford, Osprey Publishing.

Pioneer Press (1912). *Coronation Durbar 1911.* Allahabad.

Royal Archives, Windsor: RA/VIC 0 4/91. Telegram from Sir Pratab Singh 14.12.97.

RA/ GEO V N 2555 11. Anonymous Report on a visit to Jodhpur in 1923.

RA/ GEO V Q 724 78. Letter from Lord Esher to Lord Stamfordham.

Reports of the Chief Censor of Indian Mails (1914–18). Unpublished. The Oriental and India Office Library, London L/MIL/5/825, 826 and 827.

Rudolph, S.H., L.I. Rudolph, and Mohan Singh Kanota (2000). *Reversing the Gaze: Amar Singh's Diary.* New Delhi, Oxford University Press.

Singh, Dhananajaya (1996). *The House of Marwar: The Story of Jodhpur.* New Delhi, Roli Books.

Singh, Lieutenant General Hanut (1983). *'Fakhr-E-Hind': The Story of the Poona Horse.* Dehra Dun, Agrim Publishers.

Singh Sandhu, Major General G. (1981). *The Indian Cavalry: History of the Indian Armoured Corps until 1940.* New Delhi, Vision Books.

Tod, Lieutenant Colonel James (1920). *Annals and Antiquities of Rajasthan*, Volume II. London, Oxford University Press, London. First published in 1829.

War Diaries of the Jodhpur Lancers. Public Record Office, Kew: First World War: WO 95/587, WO 95/1158, WO 95/4519. Second World War: WO 169/22360, WO 169/24582 and WO 172/697.

Watson, Major General Sir H. (1930). *A Short History of the Services Rendered by the Imperial Service Troops during the Great War 1914–18.* Calcutta, Government of India Central Publications Branch.

Wheeler, S. (1991). *The History of the Delhi Coronation Durbar.* Delhi, H.K. Publishers.

Wylly, Colonel C.B. (1933). *The Poona Horse (17th QVO Cavalry)*, Volume II 1914–33. London, RUSI.

Van Wart, R.B. (1926). *The Life of Lt Gen H H Sir Pratap Singh.* London, Oxford University Press.

PHOTO CREDITS

Alamy: page 117

Archives of the Royal Palace (Brussels): pages 68–69

Eastbourne College: pages 110, 111

Flanders Field Museum: page 64

Getty Images: page 157

Imperial War Museum: pages 66, 90–91

General Amar Singh Library Museum and Trust, Castle Kanota, Jaipur: pages 19, 48, 49, 51

Karam Puri: pages 4–5, 54, 55, 100, 116, 118, 132, 152

Mary Evans Picture Library: page 131

Mehrangarh Museum Trust, Jodhpur, Rajasthan, India and His Highness Maharaja Gaj Singh II of Jodhpur: page 158

Michael Creese: pages 50, 80, 81, 83, 84, 85, 154, 155, 156

National Army Museum, Chelsea: pages 2, 10, 16

Private Collection: pages 56, 75, 76, 82

The Narpat Niwas Collection, Jodhpur. Courtesy of Rao Raja Mahendra Singh: pages 15, 30, 38, 58, 60, 72, 73, 86, 89, 95, 97, 105, 120, 121, 144–145, 192

The Royal Collection, Jodhpur. Courtesy His Highness Maharaja Gaj Singh II of Jodhpur: pages 6, 8, 22–23, 24, 27, 32, 33, 34, 35, 36–37, 39, 40–41, 42–43, 44–45, 46, 62, 71, 122–123, 124, 126–127, 128–129, 135, 136, 137, 140–141, 184–185

The Narpat Niwas Collection, Mehrangarh Museum Trust and the Royal Collection, Jodhpur, photographed by Karam Puri

The Indian Cavalry by Major General Gurcharn Singh Sandhu, Vision Books: pages 79, 106–107

Official History of the Great War Military Operations from Egypt and Palestine: Vol II Part II by Captain Cyril Falls and Major A.F. Becke, published by the Imperial War Museum: pages 92–93, 109, 113

Dalpat's Christmas card to Rao Raja and Rao Rani Narpat Singh from the Western Front in France, 1917.

ISBN: 978-81-938608-0-9

Published in India by Roli Books
M-75, Greater Kailash II Market
New Delhi-110 048, India.
Phone: ++91-11-4068 2000
Email: info@rolibooks.com
Website: www.rolibooks.com

Design: Sneha Pamneja
Layout: Naresh L. Mondal
Pre-press: Jyoti Dey
Production: Yuvraj Singh

Printed and bound in India